D1425686

£9.99

WHEN STRANGERS MARRY

Albert McDonnell

When Strangers Marry

A STUDY OF MARRIAGE BREAKDOWN IN IRELAND

306
/872

H10828

LIMERICK COUNTY LIBRARY

WITHDRAWN FROM STOCK

the columba press

First published in 1999 by
the columba press
55a Spruce Avenue, Stillorgan Industrial Park,
Blackrock, Co Dublin

Cover by Bill Bolger
Origination by The Columba Press
Printed in Ireland by Colour Books Ltd, Dublin

ISBN 185607 266 5

Copyright © 1999, Albert McDonnell

Contents

Introduction

There are very few people in Ireland who have not been touched by the pain of marriage breakdown in one way or another. Nobody goes into marriage wanting it to fail or result in separation. When a couple finds that they can no longer continue to share their lives with each other, it means that a huge part of their hopes and dreams have not been realised. The sadness and disappointment spreads far beyond the couple concerned. Obviously, the lives of their children will never be the same again. Their own parents will also share the anguish of the couple, parents suffer when they see their children suffer, and frequently their contact with their grandchildren becomes very difficult when the parents separate. The pain spreads outwards to include the relatives and friends of the couple. Separation often results in ongoing bitterness and in addition to the pain of seeing a loved one suffer, there is frequently the added danger of loosing the friendship of one or other member of the couple.

Couples begin their married life by pledging to love each other 'until death do us part'. When separation rather than death ends their life together, they themselves, their families and their friends naturally wonder why. Where did it all go wrong? There is never a simple answer and no two separated couples have exactly the same story to tell. Surveys or academic studies are not likely to give a fully satisfying explanation for marital breakdown. Human relationships are never so straightforward as to fit into the neat categories beloved by science. Yet, one of the few ways which is open to us to at least partially understand why marriages break down is by searching for common elements in the experiences of couples who separate.

My own awareness of the sadness of marital breakdown was

heightened by the experience of working with the Galway Regional Marriage Tribunal. The Galway Tribunal is one of four Regional Tribunals in Ireland which were established by the Irish Catholic Bishops in 1976 to respond to requests by separated people to have their marriages declared null. Working in the tribunal involves meeting separated people, members of their families and friends and seeking to discern why the marriages ended in separation. The people who apply to a marriage tribunal have abandoned hope of reconciliation and they come to the tribunal seeking a declaration that their marriage was invalid from the beginning. Every story was different but the most striking factor in every case was the pain and suffering that separation had brought to the couple themselves and to so many others.

This book is not an explanation of how marriage tribunals operate or how they reach their decisions. It is rather an attempt to bring together the common elements in the life-experiences of a sample of couples who applied to Galway Tribunal. In doing this a particular concern is confidentiality. People who apply to a marriage tribunal and those who help it in its work do so in confidence. Therefore, tribunal files and information contained in them are never made available to people who are not part of the tribunal. My position as a staff member of the Galway Tribunal gave me access to the tribunal archive without compromising the confidentiality of the material. In compiling this book all names and details that might serve to identify a particular person or case has been deleted. While brief, isolated quotations from the tribunal files have been used to illustrate particular points the utmost care has been taken to ensure all details that might compromise confidentiality have been omitted or radically altered. In selecting quotations only those which were typical of several cases were included and incidents which were unique or only reflected the experience of a very small number of couples are not quoted or described.

This work began as an academic thesis presented for the degree of MA in Sociology at NUI, Galway in 1998. In preparing it for publication much of the sociological theory and the more academic elements have been omitted. What remains is primarily a description of the common elements that emerged from the tribunal accounts of the life experiences of the couples in the sample. The study is not based on a random sample nor are we in a position to compare experiences of the couples in our study with the life stories of a group of couples who found happiness in marriage. However, it is about real people and their experiences in life and hopefully the description and analysis that it contains will serve to shed some light on the question of why marriages break down.

In conclusion, I wish to thank all who helped with the production of this book. In particular, my gratitude is due to Fr Michael Smyth, *Officialis* of the Galway Regional Marriage Tribunal for permitting me to base the original research on the tribunal records. I am also grateful to Frs Liam Bergin and Vincent Sherlock for their encouragement and practical help. Sr Veronica O'Looney generously gave of her time in proof-reading the printed text. I will conclude by acknowledging the people who have confronted marital breakdown at first hand: the men and women whose stories, disappointments and hopes are recounted in these pages.

List of Figures and Tables

CHAPTER ONE

Marriage in Ireland

Marriage is of central importance in the lives of Irish people. Most of us have grown up in a family based on marriage and go on to form families around a husband-wife relationship. In Ireland the dominant vision of a fulfilled life includes meeting a suitable partner and entering a life-long marriage with that person. Marriage is not only important to the individual partners, but also fulfils important tasks in society, including preparing the young for adult life, transmitting property and values and exercising social control.

Most commentaries on contemporary Irish life refer to ongoing change and transformation. Marriage has been part of this broader pattern. Many people point to current trends, especially the increased level of marriage breakdown, extramarital births and cohabiting non-marital couples, as evidence that marriage and the family are in crisis. Several high profile cases of child neglect and abuse have served to shake confidence in the well-being of family and sexual relationships. Violence towards women in the domestic situation has had a similar impact. Anti-social behaviour among young males has occasioned doubts about the effectiveness of the family as a moderating influence on socially disruptive behaviour.

The understanding of marriage held by Irish people has also changed. Marriage is increasingly viewed as a partnership involving shared decision-making. This new understanding is related to the changed position of women in society. Motherhood and career are no longer seen as mutually exclusive and women have greater opportunities to combine a full role in the labour force with family responsibility. Child-rearing is no longer regarded as exclusively the concern of the mother but is increasingly shared with the father,

creches or other non-familial facilities. The availability of contraception and abortion has made child bearing discretionary.

Despite the persistent popularity of marriage in Ireland, the
increase in marital breakdown has led to considerable debate and is
regarded as a source of concern to society and as a personal tragedy
for the couple involved and their children. Despite this concern,
very little scientific study of this trend has been carried out. Debate
on this issue has generated a lot of comment and opinion but very
little research. This has resulted in a reliance on research conducted
abroad in a different cultural context. Consequently, debate and
policy making has largely taken place in a vacuum. The purpose of
the present work is to attempt to establish some facts regarding a
sample of people whose marriages ended in separation. In this
opening chapter, we will briefly outline the evolution of the modern Irish family, current attitudes and values in Ireland regarding
sexual issues, and finally outline the present study.

EVOLUTION OF THE IRISH FAMILY

The Irish Famine of the 1840s led to the death of almost a million
people, while a similar number emigrated. After this traumatic
event, the need for economic survival became the determining factor in all other areas of life.[1] The major study of the Irish family after
the famine was undertaken by Arensberg and Kimball beginning in
1932.[2] They described a situation where the family took priority
over the individual and economic survival took precedence over all
else. The role of men, women, children and the aged were all clearly
defined; the emotional focus of the family was the mother while the
father was the decision-maker. Individual preference was accorded
little importance. A system of matchmaking gave parents a decisive
role in the selection of spouses for their children. Non-inheriting
siblings often remained on the family farm as assisting relatives, in
which case they did not marry. Sexual activity was restricted to
marriage, births outside of marriage were rare and the 'offender'
incurred considerable social censure. Children made a valuable
contribution to the labour force on farms, and marital fertility was
high. There were strong bonds of social contact and collaboration

with neighbours and kin. Economic survival and adherence to tradition were the hallmarks of the culture described by Arensberg and Kimball.

The Irish family in transition

Studies of the Irish family from the 1950s onwards contain evidence of a process of change and evolution.[3] A picture emerges of increasing dissatisfaction with the traditional approach to marriage and the family and increasing demands for change, especially from the young. Travel and contact with emigrants and the media made people aware of greater wealth and independence outside their own community. Modern means of transport and communication made parental control of socialising by the young especially difficult and ineffective. Girls particularly saw love as an essential ingredient in marriage and sought a more intimate and personal kind of marital relationship. Rural men were frequently unable to meet the expectations of women regarding marriage. The prospect of hard work, low status, a poor standard of living, a husband with a traditional concept of marriage and sharing a home with in-laws was rejected by many women in favour of emigration. Ownership of land, which was previously a virtual guarantee of marriage, now made marriage less likely. These studies depict traditional society as fighting for its survival.

A study published in 1977[4] categorised a sample of farm families in the West of Ireland into six cluster groups according to their task roles and decision-making patterns. These clusters varied from the traditional to a 'modern middle class' type with an emphasis on partnership, joint decision-making and low segregation in task roles. About ⅓ of the families resembles the traditional type; ¼ resemble the most 'modern' type; and the balance was somewhere in between. The authors concluded that:

> The marital relationship has become increasingly based on emotionally supportive bonds built up between couples in the courtship and early marriage stage, and has been moving away from the almost instrumental basis of the relationship which appeared to be characteristic of traditional marriages.[5]

These authors also found that changes in values and expectations are not always translated into changes in behaviour. This is of particular relevance to levels of dissatisfaction within marriage. Frequently women had modern attitudes and expectations of marriage while their husbands retained more traditional views. In many marriages the traditional approach prevailed and wives were frequently dissatisfied and conflict resulted.

The dramatic changes that occurred in the Irish family are evident in studies conducted from the 1970s onwards. These studies focused on issues such as unmarried mothers and child abuse or neglect.[6] A new vision of family is evident in the way one author defines the term to include lone parents, cohabiting couples, as well as married couples.[7] A study of single parenthood saw it as a threat to the norm of bearing children within a marital relationship. These studies contain convincing evidence of diversity within Irish attitudes and behaviour regarding sexual activity, child-bearing, and of a less effective process of passing on traditional attitudes and codes of behaviour.

Marriage breakdown

Relatively little research has been conducted into the causes or nature of marriage breakdown in Ireland. In this section, we shall survey such research as has been conducted and supplement it with reference to the reports of counselling and other agencies concerned with marriage breakdown.

One of the few research-based studies of marriage breakdown in Ireland was published by Kathleen O'Higgins in 1974.[8] Her objectives were to study the marital situation which led some men to choose desertion and to identify causes of breakdown. She terms her study 'exploratory' and does not claim that her sample is representative. Regarding the pre-marriage period, O'Higgins' study pointed to the poor level of communication within couples. She concludes that:

> ... communication for our couples was low ... they had not used their courtship as a learning experience, they were acting out a process of getting to know one another, by going out together ... They were ... merely going through the motions.[9]

Regarding factors such as pregnancy, short courtships and dysfunctional family backgrounds, which are frequently seen as predictive of marital breakdown, O'Higgins' study is non-conclusive.
The poor level of communication found in the courtship continued
in the marriage. The couples tended not to discuss matters such as
the preferred size of their family or even the husband's earnings.
O'Higgins' subjects had larger than average families and the wives
frequently sought compensation in their children for the poor
nature of the marital relationship. Husbands tended to have little
involvement in the rearing of children and the study supports the
view that the husbands felt excluded from the family group and
sought consolation in drink or adultery. Excessive alcohol consumption by the husband was common, though violence was
rarely significant. The presence of children restricted the couple's
joint social life. O'Higgins found a reticence among her subjects to
discuss the sexual aspect of marriage. However, she concluded that
sexual difficulties arose from a deteriorating relationship and in
turn led to a further deterioration of the broader relationship. Most
of the women believed that there were problems present from the
beginning of their marriages. O'Higgins sees a link between marriage breakdown and more general social failure.

O'Higgins' study indicates that the Irish experience of desertion
tends to reflect world-wide patterns. She regards desertion as the
result of the piling up of adverse circumstances. Psychological factors and the absence of preparation or relevant education are likely
explanations as to why some marriages sustain strains and others
do not. She states:

> The relationship ... was unable to support stress from sources
> such as false ideas of what marriage would be like, marriage
> forced by pregnancy, poor sexual relationship, inadequate edu-
> cation for life in general and marriage in particular.[10]

O'Higgins' study is helpful in that it illustrates the changing nature
of Irish marriage in the 1970s, especially the increasing emphasis on
emotional factors, reduced social support and a growing acceptance of separation as an option.

The experience of counselling and mediation services

O'Higgins' focus on communication as an issue in marriage is reflected in the experiences of counselling and mediation services. The problem of communication dominated the reports of all agencies. Counselling resulted in an improved relationship in a significant number of cases. However, a large minority of clients separated. The agencies' records indicate that their clients made considerable efforts to save their marriages. The profile of marriages under stress that emerges from these reports reflects the modern day emphasis on personal fulfilment. Personal choice plays a major role in relationships and couples view separation as a logical reaction to a disappointing experience of marriage. The subjective analysis of the people who have experienced unhappy marriages emphasises factors such as lack of communication and emotional intimacy. While individual and psychological factors play a role in the inability of people to cope with adversity in marriage, societal factors are also significant. Family of origin, nature of the courtship, the presence and timing of children, the age of the partners, their relative social, occupational and educational status, and financial and recreational patterns, are among the factors emerging from this section as associated with marriage breakdown.

A Galway based study of marriage breakdown[11] concluded that the process leading to separation is complex. In most cases, several factors combined to bring about breakdown. These factors included: pre-marital pregnancy; short courtships; early marriages and dysfunctional families of origin. Within marriage, alcoholism was found to be frequently associated with domestic violence and pre-marital pregnancy and was much more common among men. It was also the most frequently cited reason for an unhappy childhood in families of origin. Heavy drinking, when habitual in teenagehood, often went unnoticed in courtship. Extramarital affairs were most common among men and were usually preceded by lengthy dysfunctional marriages and emerged as primarily a symptom rather than a cause of marital problems.

Conclusion

During the present century, considerable change has taken place in the Irish family and in marriage patterns. A structure designed to ensure economic survival has evolved into one more responsive to the emotive needs of the participants. Marriage has increasingly become a private affair and parental control of the timing of marriage and spousal selection has virtually disappeared. Segregation of roles within marriage has declined and married couples now live more private lives in their own accommodation. The dominant position of marriage has declined and sexual relationships and child-bearing have ceased to be the preserve of married couples. Expectations of marriage have altered radically: personal fulfilment has emerged as the major criterion by which marriage is now evaluated. Factors such as dysfunctional family of origin, short courtships, early marriage, personality problems or addictions were identified as having a possible association with marital instability. Within marriage, failure in communication and a lack of emotional warmth in the relationship emerged as the key issues.

CONTEXT OF PRESENT IRISH FAMILY

A society in transformation

The evolution of the Irish family from an institution based on precedent and the imperative for economic survival, to one more responsive to the individual and emotional needs of its participants, did not take place in isolation. To appreciate the changes which we have described above it is helpful to see them in the context of the changes which occurred in the broader society.

The post-1945 period saw immense change in most areas of Irish life. The economy became more open to international influences, particularly after Ireland joined the Common Market[12] in 1973. Farming became more commercial and mechanised and required less manual labour. The development of foreign owned and indigenous industry provided an option to farming, emigration or permanent celibacy and low status as an assisting relative on the family farm. This resulted in greater numbers having the option of marriage in Ireland. The media explosion took hold and television rivalled the fireside as the focus of many homes. Censorship was relaxed and ideas from abroad increasingly permeated Irish society. Patterns of social life changed as ease of transport and an increase in disposable income facilitated greater choice in leisure and socialising. The clearly defined and separate roles of the sexes declined in favour of an equal-opportunities ethos. The participation rate of married women in the labour force increased dramatically. The Catholic Church also experienced change, most notably in the reforms agreed at the Second Ecumenical Vatican Council, 1962-1965. A decline in church attendance, coupled with increasing rejection of church teaching, particularly regarding sexual matters, became apparent.[13] Education became available to greater numbers as the present century proceeded. While emigration rates ebbed and flowed, the increasing ease of travel and communication served to increase the influence that emigrants had on their home communities. The role of the state expanded, most notably in healthcare, child welfare, housing and social welfare. By the 1990s Irish family structures existed in a radically different context from the one which had served to mould them.

Demographic changes

Dramatic change occurred in the major measurable indicators of Irish family life. The marriage rate increased dramatically in the 1960s, and in the 1970s declined somewhat in line with general European trends.[14] The age at which people married followed a similar pattern: a decline commenced in the 1950s and continued until 1977, when the average age at the time of marriage was 26.2 years for men and 24 years for women. Again, in line with European trends age at the time of marriage increased after 1977. A drop of 37% occurred in the average family size between 1961 and 1981 and this decline has continued. The increasing use of contraception and the rising economic cost of children are regarded as being associated with the drop in fertility within marriage. Various studies provided evidence of a general acceptance and use of all methods of family planning.[15] Paradoxically, births outside marriage increased dramatically[16] to reach 19.5% of total births in

1993.[17] Adoption declined dramatically as a solution to unwanted pregnancy as pregnant Irish women increasingly availed of abortion facilities in England. Census data indicates that cohabitation outside of marriage is becoming increasingly common. The rate of marriage breakdown and separation has also increased. A recent study concluded that the Irish rate of marriage breakdown is broadly in line with that of the predominant Catholic countries of Southern Europe.[18]

In summarised recent demographic trends in Ireland, commentators speak of a process of Europeanisation.[19] Most of the distinctive features of the earlier Irish family have disappeared or become less pronounced as Ireland increasingly reflects broader European patterns.

Values and behaviour

Another area of change in Irish society relates to values, particularly regarding marriage and the family. In 1968 an American commentator observed that:

> The impression of total Catholicism can begin on the flight to Dublin, for if it is an Aer Lingus plane it will be named after a saint … there appear to be churches at every turn … the Irish churches are busy places … the book shops are full of religious works. The newspapers tell of the thousands of pilgrims who have climbed Croagh Patrick or of the hundreds flying off to Lourdes.[20]

In 1990, the situation appears very differently to an Irish bishop:

> There is a worrying decline in the level of belief, especially with regard to those truths which are most difficult to reconcile with contemporary ideas.[21]

Surveys of religious practice underline the bishop's point. Figure 1.1 presents data from surveys of weekly, or more frequent attendance at Mass, between 1973 and 1995.[22]

A study of the 1990 European Values Survey showed that Ireland is becoming more like the rest of Europe regarding the role of religion in life.[23] The study referred to a number of factors associ-

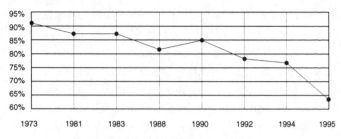

Figure 1.1 Weekly Attendance at Mass

ated with the emergence of a new Irish Catholicism: a focus on a life force, rather than a personal God; a questioning of the church's right to speak authoritatively on personal morality or government policy; support for the church's role in social[24] issues; liberal attitudes on sexual matters; and an optimistic view of access to salvation. Demographic changes and the widespread use of contraception are often seen as indicative of the loss of authority by the church and the end of the traditional alliance between the church and women.

The factors discussed above indicate a move towards greater freedom of individual choice and an increased emphasis on personal satisfaction. Though a high level of spiritual consciousness persists, liturgical practice and observance of church teaching on matters of private morality has declined. Religion is accorded a considerably reduced role in determining values and behaviour, particularly regarding sexual issues and relationships.

Legislative changes

Demographic and social change in Ireland has been accompanied by changes in the law. The 1937 Constitution reflected aspects of Catholic teaching, particularly regarding the family and the mother's role in the home. However, judicial interpretation of the Constitution from the 1960s onwards emphasised personal rights. Legislative change also enlarged the individual's freedom of choice. This was evident in measures such as the decriminalisation of homosexual relations between consenting adults, the virtual elimination of restrictions on the sale of contraceptives to adults, the abolition of the status of illegitimacy, and the provision of financial support for single mothers. Abortion provoked a major debate and, notwithstanding a 1983 referendum prohibiting its introduction, the trend of constitutional change in the 1990s favoured individual choice. The role of women in work and society was addressed in the removal of restrictions on the employment of married women in the state service, the introduction of equal pay and the protection of the succession rights of wives. Marriage breakdown was dealt with by measures dealing with the protection and maintenance of spouses and children, provisions which facilitated marital separation, and the 1996 constitutional amendment which facilitated the introduction of divorce. The unifying thread running through the various manifestations of change in Irish society is an increasing emphasis on the individual, his/her rights and personal fulfilment. Increasing acceptance of outside influences, legal changes, demographic shifts and changes in attitudes, all converge on the freedom to exercise choice as the dominant value. This corresponds with the modern concept of marriage and family as described in recent Irish studies.

Conclusion

Marriage is now regarded by most Irish people as primarily an affective/emotional relationship. Many of the economic, social, education and welfare functions that the family previously provided are now fulfilled by the state or other extra-familial institutions. Marriage has lost its virtual monopoly on sexual activity, childbearing, and cohabiting relationships. People enter and leave marriage increasingly in line with their personal preference rather than external, legal, social or moral imperatives. When the reality of marriage does not meet the expectations of one or both participants, the option of leaving is chosen more readily than previously. Increasingly, a particular marriage will survive or fall in so far as it fulfils the emotional needs of the participants. The role played by social, religious and economic factors in supporting marriage has declined.

NATURE OF THE STUDY

One of the problems in researching marriage breakdown is the diffi-

H10828

culty in accumulating the necessary data. Original research requires considerable resources and therefore is relatively rare. This study of marriage breakdown is based on a source of information that has not been previously used in Ireland.

The Galway Regional Marriage Tribunal

In 1976 the Irish Catholic Church established four regional marriage tribunals to deal with the growing number of applications from people in broken marriages to have their marriages investigated with a view to the possible granting of a decree of nullity. Prior to 1976, each individual diocese dealt with applications from its own area. In processing applications, these tribunals accumulate and retain a vast amount of information concerning the individuals involved, their family background and the courtship and marriage. In addition to its use in the decision-making process regarding the application for a decree of nullity, this information can also be used to expand our understanding of marriage breakdown.

The present study is based on a sample drawn from the cases processed by the Galway Regional Marriage Tribunal. The Galway Tribunal, based in Galway city, serves the eight Western Catholic dioceses of Galway, Clonfert, Tuam, Killaloe, Ardagh and Clonmacnoise, Achonry, Killala, and Elphin. This area includes the entire province of Connacht, almost all Clare, Longford, North Tipperary and South and West Offaly and small areas in Westmeath, Cavan, Laois and Limerick. A Catholic population of 553,682 live in the region.[25] Most of the marriages investigated by the Galway Tribunal were celebrated within the region served by the tribunal and almost all applications are received from Catholics. However, occasionally applications are received from non-Catholics who had been married previously and who now wish to marry a Catholic and to have that marriage recognised by the Catholic Church.

The processing of applications by the tribunal involves interviewing each party and witnesses nominated by them. The person who applies (known as the petitioner) is invited for an interview, at which the circumstances of the marriage and the consequent problems are discussed. The other party (the respondent) is then offered the opportunity of presenting his/her perspective on the marriage to the tribunal. In about 75% of the cases the respondent avails of this opportunity. Both parties are invited to nominate witnesses for interview by the tribunal. Witnesses should know one or both parties well and be knowledgeable about the courtship and/or the marriage. Reports may also be received from marriage counsellors, medical doctors, psychologists or other professionals who had contact with the couple regarding their marriage. The tribunal judges study the transcripts of the interviews with each party, the witnesses and the various reports and make a decision on the application. An appeal procedure is available to those who receive a negative decision, while an affirmative decision must be confirmed by another tribunal.

Each year Galway Regional Marriage Tribunal receives between 100 and 140 applications, though not all applicants persevere with their cases. Each case contains between sixty and one hundred pages of evidence. The sample chosen for this study is provided by the cases received by the Galway Tribunal in 1993. In that year, Galway Regional Marriage Tribunal received 136 applications, of which 80 resulted in a decision by the Galway Tribunal.[26] The year 1993 was chosen as it is the most recent year for which the process of collecting evidence is complete. The applications received by Galway Tribunal in a particular year concern marriages celebrated over a wide range of years.

The questionnaires used in interviewing the petitioner, the respondent and the witnesses focus on three main areas. These are: (1) Background – the family of origin of each party, his/her school and work records and previous relationships (if any). (2) Courtship: how the couple met; the nature of their courtship; their expectations of marriage; the degree to which they discussed and planned their future; pressures on the couples to marry and/or advice against marriage; doubts regarding marriage; interruptions to the courtship; and specific problems regarding violence, alcohol, infidelity, sex, finance, communication, etc. (3) Marriage: the couple's initial adaptation to married life; adjustment to parenthood; sexual relationship; financial issues; accommodation; social life; relations with family, friends; nature of problems encountered; attempts to address the problems; the circumstances of the final separation; major events in the lives of both parties since the breakdown.

The absence of civil divorce in Ireland had created the *de facto* situation whereby the only method by which a failed marriage could formally be declared over, and the option of a future marriage secured, was by applying to a Catholic Marriage tribunal. Civil nullity was available in Ireland as a High Court procedure. However, it was costly, the jurisprudence employed was restrictive, and applications were relatively few. Provision also existed for the recognition of civil divorces secured abroad. This required the establishment of a domicile abroad and therefore was available to few people. Judicial separation is available in civil law, but does not facilitate remarriage. People who received church declarations of nullity could marry in church. However, unless the previously married party secured a civil dissolution or a civil declaration of nullity of his/her marriage, the civil authorities continued to regard the original marriage as valid. The state rarely if ever enforced the law regarding bigamy in these situations. However, many people appeared happy with church recognition of a second union, even when it was not accompanied by state recognition or protection.

The information accumulated by the Marriage Tribunal focuses on the lived experience of marriage of the couples involved. In line with normal procedure, we will not reveal the identity of the parties to any individual marriage or the identities of witnesses or professionals who provided evidence or reports. The records of the Galway Marriage Tribunal are confidential and all interviews are conducted on that basis. While quotations from cases will be used to illustrate particular points, great care is taken not to disclose the identity of the couple involved or the person quoted. This necessitates the omission of proper names and the alteration of other details which might betray identities. However, in all cases the point relevant to the study will be preserved in the illustrative quotations used.

Limitations to the study

Our study is primarily descriptive and allows us to identify common trends and patterns. Certain limitations necessarily apply. The non-inclusion of a group of comparative couples who did not separate reduces the value of this research. If we were to compare our sample with such a group, a clearer picture of the possible causes of marriage breakdown would emerge. Another possible limitation is the fact that we are using data which was collected for another purpose, i.e. deciding if the marriages concerned can be declared null and void. However, the interview technique used by the tribunal ensures that the information collected is detailed and broad ranging. Catholic tribunal decisions have no ramifications regarding children or property and therefore the focus is primarily on the circumstances of the marriage.

The reliability of the information given to the Galway Marriage Tribunals is also an important point.[27] Many separated Irish Catholics wish to enter a new marriage in church and may be tempted to use subterfuge to attain a decree of nullity. Applicants may invent or exaggerate evidence which they believe will increase their chances of receiving a decree of nullity, and it is not inconceivable that some petitioners may seek to coach witnesses. Marriage breakdown is often accompanied by bitterness between the couple and some respondents may seek to frustrate their former spouse's attempt to secure a decree of nullity. This sabotage could take the form of the respondent testifying that the breakdown of the marriage was due to a factor which would not qualify as a basis for the granting of such a decree. Furthermore, in speaking to a Catholic Marriage tribunal there may be a tendency on the part of people to present themselves as morally virtuous by avoiding mention of behaviour such as extramarital sexual relations or abortion, which are disapproved of by the church.

Several factors serve to counteract the points outlined above. Tribunal interviews are conducted under oath and it is reasonable to assume that people who apply to a Church tribunal are likely to regard an oath as a serious matter. The tribunal does not conduct its affairs in an adversarial manner and the object is to arrive at the truth rather than apportion blame. The uncorroborated testimony of an individual is not accepted by the tribunal and, in addition to interviewing both parties, evidence is received from witnesses and professionals. A prerequisite to the granting of a decision by the tribunal is the establishment of the salient facts. In the absence of independent testimony which is capable of resolving contradictory statements by the parties, the application is unlikely to proceed to the decision-making stage. While there are always inherent difficulties in guaranteeing the veracity of evidence presented to any forum, the above factors support the credibility of evidence presented to Marriage Tribunals.

Another difficulty lies in the fact that our sample is limited in that it only includes people who opted to apply to the tribunal and their spouses. Non-Catholics and non-religious people are underrepresented among applications to Catholic Church Tribunals. Also, some separated Catholics who do not apply to the tribunal may not wish to enter a new relationship or to seek church approval for such a relationship. Furthermore, some separated people, since they perceive a decree of nullity as a statement that their marriage never existed and as contradictory of their lived experience, do not apply. While these points impact on the nature and the number of applications received by the tribunal, special circumstances prevailing in Ireland serve as a counterweight. Church attendance remains high and therefore Irish people are more likely that their European counterparts to desire church recognition for a second union. In 1993, when our sample members applied to the tribunal, the absence of civil divorce effectively deprived separated people of a secular means to terminate their marriages. For many people, Catholic Tribunals filled this void and provided a means of entering a new marriage. These factors are likely to increase the number of applications received by the tribunal and improve the representative nature of our sample.

The fact that not all broken marriages meet the criteria set by the Catholic Church for nullity also impacts on the representative nature of our sample. The church recognises that valid marriages can end in separation, usually due to a lack of effort or the deliberate decision of one or other party. These cases are usually rejected at an early stage by the tribunal and are not included in our sample. This serves to remove a category of broken marriages from our sample. Another limitation is that about 20%–25% of respondents do not co-operate with the tribunal. The evidence of witnesses, some of whom will have known the respondent well, helps compensate for this limitation. The study is also limited in geographical terms. However, while the region served by the Galway Tribunal is generally rural, it also includes the city of Galway and large towns such as Ennis, Athlone and Sligo, as well as numerous smaller towns and villages. This urban-rural mix enhances the representative nature of the study.

Despite the limitations outlined above, a study of tribunal records will expand our understanding of marriage breakdown. While our sample source is limited, yet it is likely to be representative of a substantial segment of separated couples in Ireland.

Conclusion

Marriage is now understood in Ireland as a relationship designed to bring personal happiness to the participants. Many of the economic, social, education and welfare functions that the family previously provided are now fulfilled by the state or other extra-familial institutions. Marriage has lost its virtual monopoly on sexual activity, childbearing and cohabiting relationships. People enter and leave marriage increasingly in line with their personal preference. When the reality of marriage does not meet the expectations of one or both participants, the option of leaving is chosen more readily than previously. Increasingly, a particular marriage will survive or fall in so far as it fulfils the emotional needs of the participants. In the following chapters we shall examine the accounts of marriages provided by our sample couples and their witnesses and seek to establish trends and factors common to their various experiences of marriage.

CHAPTER TWO

Profile of Sample Couples

Before discussing our couples' experiences of marriage in detail, we will present a profile of our sample members in statistical form. The records of the Galway Regional Marriage Tribunal contain considerable information which can be presented in percentage or chart form. This material includes age at time of marriage, geographic origin, social class, educational standard, duration of courtship, length of marriage, number of children, subsequent relationships, employment status, and recourse to counsellors. The statistical data contained in this chapter will act as a framework into which the more detailed descriptive and analytical material contained in later chapters will fit.

OVERVIEW

In 1993, 136 people approached Galway Marriage Tribunal to have their marriages investigated with a view to the possible granting of a decree of nullity. By February 1997, eighty of these cases had been concluded with a judgement granted by the Tribunal. Based on the experience of previous years, it is unlikely that more than a tiny minority of the remaining cases will ever reach conclusion. The reasons why applications are discontinued vary from the absence of a *prima facie*[1] case to a loss of interest by the petitioner. This loss of interest is usually due either to the ending of a relationship which he/she had hoped would lead to marriage or to disenchantment caused by the detailed nature of the Tribunal procedure.

Our sample consists of the eighty 1993 cases which were presented for judgement in Galway. In sixty-four (80%) cases both parties co-operated and were interviewed by the Tribunal. Even in cases where the respondent chooses not to take part in the proceedings the tribunal records contain substantial information regarding the respondent. While the source of this information is frequently the petitioner, information regarding the respondent is also corroborated by witnesses, some of whom may be members of his/her family or circle of friends. The focus of the investigation is the marriage itself and therefore the Tribunal endeavours to construct a detailed picture of the role played by both parties in the union. Therefore, it is possible to include both parties under all headings used in this descriptive chapter.

Initiative and response

Organisations working in the area of marriage breakdown report that women are more likely than men to seek outside help regarding a dysfunctional marriage. In the present study, 61.25% of petitioners are female.[2] The high level of co-operation among respondents (80%) served to redress this gender imbalance among petitioners. Taking petitioners and respondents together, 144 spouses co-operated with the Tribunal of whom 75 (52%) were women and 69 (48%) were men. Sixteen respondents (five women and eleven men) did not co-operate with the Tribunal. Figure 2.1 summarises this information.

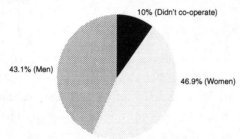

Figure 2.1 Petitioners and Respondents
Analysis by Gender

This high level of gender balance enhances our study by ensuring that the perspectives of both men and women are adequately represented.

Sample members prior to marriage

The first section of the questionnaires used in interviewing petitioners, respondents and witnesses focuses on the family, on the educational

and work background of each party and on their courtship. These
factors are important influences in shaping the individual's expectations of marriage and therefore are of interest in this study.

Geographical origins

The members of our study rarely ventured far beyond their own
home area in seeking a marriage partner. In 81% of cases both partners grew up within a twenty mile radius of each other. Of the
remainder, half were between partners from different parts of
Ireland and half involved one partner from Ireland and the other
from the USA or Great Britain. Ireland, Britain and the United
States are the only countries of origin represented in our study.
Figure 2.2 present this information.

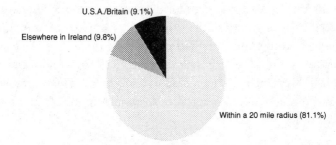

Figure 2.2 Origin of Parties to Marriages

Even foreign-born members of our sample frequently had
strong family links with Ireland. Only four couples involved a person whose parents were not born in Ireland. One member of the
Irish community in Britain married a local person, two British people living in Ireland married an Irish partner, and an Irish immi-
grant married an American. Most marriages in our study involving
a foreign-born partner resulted from an Irish person emigrating to
England and marrying a member of the Irish community there. The
Travelling Community was the only ethnic minority represented in
our study; in one marriage both members were Travellers. No racial
minority was represented in the study. All members of the sample
were Catholic except for three British-born people.

The overall picture that emerges is one of homogeneity.[3] Even
those who married outside their own geographical areas usually

married people very like themselves, members of the Irish Catholic community in Britain. In summary, the members of our sample overwhelmingly married people who resembled themselves in ethnic, racial, national, religious and even geographical terms.

Educational attainment

The tribunal files contain information on the educational standard reached by the parties to the marriages which it investigates. Consequently it is possible to assign a category on a scale of educational attainment to each person in the sample. The following seven-point scale was constructed to accommodate the relevant data (cf. Figure 2.3).

Point One represents incomplete primary education.

Point Two – completed primary education.

Point Three – those who left second level education without sitting state examinations.

Point Four – Intermediate or Group Certificate qualification.

Point Five – Leaving Certificate qualification.

Point Six – Post Leaving Certificate (non-degree) academic qualification.

Point Seven – University Degree qualification.

Considering men and women together, 5.1% received primary level education only; 75.64% had some secondary education, and

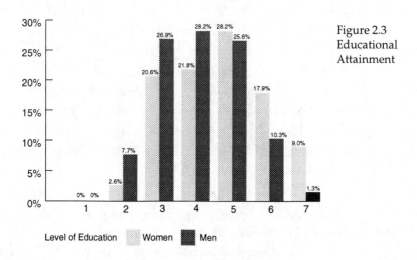

Figure 2.3
Educational
Attainment

Level of Education   Women   Men

19.2% had tertiary education. Using our seven point scale, the average education level reached was 4.1 for men and 4.6 for women. In 47.5% of marriages the wife had a higher level of education than her husband, while the reverse was true in 17.5% of cases. In 35% of marriages both parties had the same level of education, and in a further 39.7% of cases, both parties occupied contiguous places on our scale. While wives tended to be better educated than their husbands, the difference was rarely more than one point on our scale. Allowing for this caveat, our survey points to significant homogeneity in educational standard, within individual marriages.

Social class and employment

The Tribunal files record the occupation of each spouse at the time of marriage. Figure 2.4 presents this information using the following six-point scale taken from the 1986 Census of Population.

Social Class I – Higher Professional.
Social Class II – Lower Professional.
Social Class III – Other Non-Manual.
Social Class IV – Skilled Manual.
Social Class V – Semi-skilled Manual.
Social Class VI – Unskilled Manual.

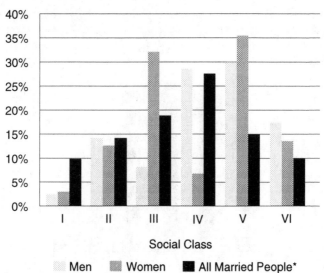

Social Class

Men   Women   All Married People*

* *Population distribution for all married persons as contained in 1986 Census.*

Figure 2.4 Social Class

All members of our sample were or had been in employment prior to marriage and can be assigned to a class on our scale. The high representation of women in Social Class III (other non-manual) reflects the inclusion of typists, book-keepers and clerical workers in this category. Inversely, the large presence of men in Social Class IV (skilled manual) is due to the inclusion of male dominated occupations such as gardeners, fishermen, mine and quarry workers, mechanics and plumbers in this category. As Figure 2.5 shows, 33% of spouses belonged to the same social class; in 37% of cases the wife came from a higher social class, while the reverse was true in the balance of cases.

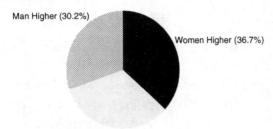

Figure 2.5 Social Class in Marriage
Comparison within Marriages

Our subjects' tendency to marry within the same or similar social groups is demonstrated by the fact that in 71% of marriages the parties came from the same or contiguous social class groups. The patterns of homogeneity in educational standard are repeated in relation to social class.

Information on the employment status of the parties was recorded only in relation to the time when the application to the tribunal was initiated. The members of the sample fall into four categories: in employment, unemployed, engaged in home duties, or retired (cf. Figure 2.6). The category of 'home duties' is confined to women, though six men combined custody of children with paid employment outside the home. The available information does not permit a calculation of the number of women engaged in home duties who would welcome paid employment outside the home. In summary: 77.6% of men were in employment, 19.7% unemployed, and 2.6%

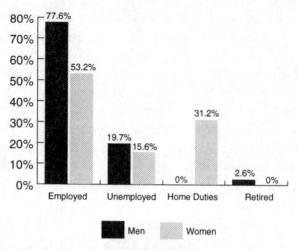

Figure 2.6 Employment Status
at time of application to Tribunal

retired. Among women, 53.2% were in paid employment, 15.6% unemployed, and 31.2% engaged in home duties.[4] The labour force participation rate for separated women in our study is considerably higher than that for women in the appropriate age groups in the general population. Many women who had the option of being a fulltime homemaker in marriage were compelled by financial need to find paid employment after the separation.

Place of meeting

The largest group (40%) of couples in our sample first met at a disco or nightclub or, in the case of the older couples, dances or marquees. The next largest group (16.3%) met through work or school. Social activities, principally sport, leisure activities and youth clubs, were the occasion of 13.8% of couples meeting, while only 3.8% of couples referred to meeting in a pub. Some couples (3.8%) grew up in the same neighbourhood and friendship developed into courtship. A residual category accounts for 7.5%. This includes a couple who met through a newspaper, getting in touch column, and three couples who met on holiday. The figure of 15% for couples who were introduced by friends appears low and may involve overlap with other groups. Many introductions are likely to have

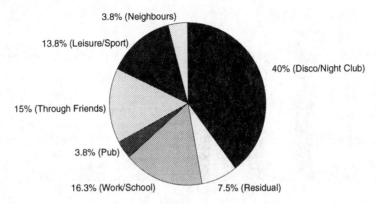

Figure 2.7 Place of Meeting

taken place at work, in a pub or at a social function and therefore may be included in these other categories. The dominant role played by social outlets in the process of meeting a prospective spouse is confirmed by Figure 2.7 and highlights the contrast with the traditional method of matchmaking.

Sexual aspects of courtship

The trend towards greater sexual involvement prior to marriage is confirmed by the present study. Fifty-one couples (63.7%) stated that their courtship involved sexual intercourse. Cohabitation prior to marriage was less common: twenty-two couples (27.5%) lived together during courtship. A premarital pregnancy occurred in thirty cases, representing 37.5% of the sample.

Sixteen women (20%) gave birth prior to marriage; seven pre-marital births involved partners other than their future husband. Information regarding the number of men who fathered children with partners other than their future wives is not recorded. There is no reference to a child born as a result of a premarital pregnancy being offered for adoption. Four premarital pregnancies were con-cluded by abortion. However, the accuracy of the figures regarding abortion is open to question. In view of the church's opposition to induced abortion, a certain reserve in disclosing a termination to the Tribunal is likely. In one case the only mention of an abortion occurred in a professional report supplied in confidence to the

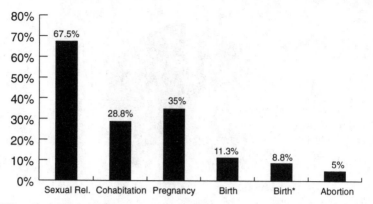

*Women who had children with a partner other than their future husband, before
marriage.*

Figure 2.8 Sexual Aspects of Courtship

Tribunal. In other cases one party mentioned that an abortion was
procured on condition that the matter not be discussed with the
other party. However, the overwhelming impression is that the
majority of couples in this sample choose marriage rather than
abortion as a strategy for dealing with an unplanned pregnancy.
Figure 2.8 presents our findings on the sexual aspects of courtship.

When the couples who married during or after 1986 are considered separately, the statistics regarding sexual involvement alter
dramatically. Figure 2.9 contrasts the pre-1986 marriages with those
which took place in 1986 and afterwards and shows increased incidence of premarital sexual involvement. Premarital sexual involve-

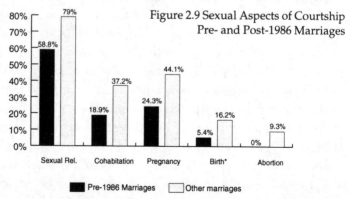

Figure 2.9 Sexual Aspects of Courtship
Pre- and Post-1986 Marriages

*Includes women who had children by a partner other than their future husband
before marriage.*

ment occurred in 79% of marriages celebrated during or after 1986; 37.2% of these couples cohabited prior to marriage and 44.1% experienced premarital pregnancy. All the abortions in the study occur in the context of the more recent marriages. The trend evident in Figure 2.9 supports the contention that sexual involvement prior to marriage is increasingly becoming the norm.

Religious practice

The Tribunal invites the petitioner to comment on the religious practice of each party prior to marriage. The reply to this question usually takes the form of brief statement indicating whether each party practiced his/her religion regularly. The respondent and the witnesses frequently include reference to the religious practice of both parties in their evidence. The extremely high level of internal consistency in each case concerning this point is impressive and indicates that a high level of accuracy may be presumed. While the use of only two categories to present this data (those who attended church regularly and those who did not) is somewhat crude, it does provide an insight into our subjects.

Of the eighty marriages in our study, seventy-seven were between Catholics and three involved one non-Catholic partner. The non-Catholics were all British Protestants and all three are described as non-practising. The overall practice rate for the sample was 68.1%. Men had a lower practice rate (67.9%) than the women in the study (71.8%). In 85.7% of couples at least one partner attended church regularly, in 55.8% of couples both parties attended church habitually, and in 11% neither party attended regularly. Since the marriages concerned were celebrated over a thirty year period, a comparison between our sample and national surveys of religious practice is not feasible. Almost half our couples got married (45%) between 1986 and 1990. The men in this group showed a significant drop in religious practice (59.4%), though the figure for women indicates a slight increase (73%). National surveys of religious practice for the period from 1986 to 1990 indicate overall levels of practice of between 81.6% and 85%.[5] Since the records for previous decades indicate even higher levels of religious practice, it is evident that the people in our study were significantly less likely than the overall population to attend church regularly. However this finding may be influenced by the dominance of people in their early twenties in our sample who tend to have a lower than average practice rate.[6]

Age at time of marriage

Our couples were relatively young on entry into marriage. Their ages ranged from 16 to 57 years; the average being 24.4 years. Following the traditional pattern, women married earlier than men, their average age being 22.7 years as opposed to 26 years for men.[7] In 71.2% of our sample marriages the husband was older than his wife; the reverse was true in 12.5% of cases. Premarital pregnancy tended to depress the age at marriage by two years for women and 1.75 years for men.[8]

Duration of courtship

Duration of courtship ranged from six months to ten years: the average being 3.14 years. Where a premarital pregnancy occurred the average duration of the courtship dropped to 2.8 years, though this was inflated by one couple's decision to marry after a ten year courtship in the context of a premarital pregnancy. Figure 2.10 presents a comparison between couples who experienced a premarital pregnancy and those which did not.

The representative nature of our findings in supported by Figure 2.11 which illustrates the marked similarity between the length of courtships experienced by Murphy's subjects and the equivalent data in our study. The wide variation in duration of courtship in our sample supports Murphy's conclusion that 'a long courtship is not an infallible indicator for a successful marriage'.[9]

Conclusion

In theory, apart from restrictions such as incest, the manner of selection of a spouse in Ireland is entirely free. However, as our sample illustrates, people overwhelmingly marry within their own social, ethnic, religious and geographical group. This pattern reflects trends prevalent in most other societies and is explicable in that people tend to meet and socialise with those who live near their own area of residence and share common interests and friends. Our

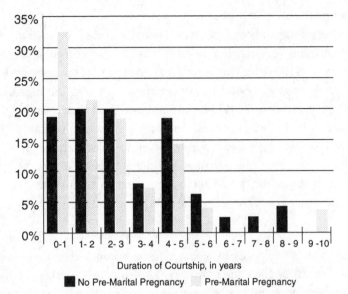

Duration of Courtship, in years

■ No Pre-Marital Pregnancy ░ Pre-Marital Pregnancy

The cases represented on the left are those which did not experience a premarital pregnancy, while the cases on the right involved pregnancy prior to marriage.

Figure 2.10 Duration of Courtship
Role of Pre-Marital Pregnancy

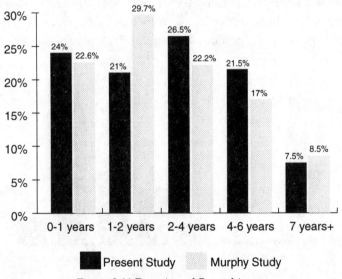

■ Present Study ░ Murphy Study

Figure 2.11 Duration of Courtship
Comparison with Murphy study

findings show that in selecting a marriage partner people continue to attach importance to factors such as social class, education, occupation, age, geographic origin, religious affiliation and ethnic group. It is likely that factors outside the range of the present study, such as personality and physical appearance, also impinge on the selection of a spouse. While a romantic concept of marriage is dominant in Irish society, considerations such as love operate in conjunction with the more tangible issues discussed above. The view that the selection of a marriage partner is in effect a process of balancing the qualities possessed by each partner against those desired by the other is supported by the data presented here.

DURING AND AFTER MARRIAGE

The subject's experience of marriage is recounted in detail in the Tribunal files. The issue of the breakdown of the marriage and how both partners fared post-separation is also addressed. In this section, we shall focus on those aspects of their relationship during and after the marriage which are open to representation in statistical form.

Timescale and duration of marriage

The marriages in our study were celebrated between 1963 and 1992 with almost half married between 1986 and 1990. Figure 2.12 details the percentage of couples who married in each five year period.

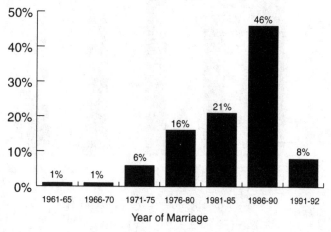

Figure 2.12 Year of Marriage

Most couples who applied to the Tribunal in 1993 had separated within the previous three years. Fifty-eight couples (72.5% of the total) who applied in 1993 had separated between 1990 and 1992. Three couples who separated during the early weeks of 1993 had their application accepted during December 1993. Figure 2.13 presents the data regarding year of separation.

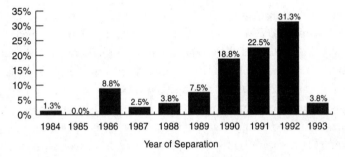

Figure 2.13 Year of Separation

Figure 2.14 summaries the data concerning the length of the marriages in our sample. The average duration was 6.2 years; the range being from 27 years to under six months. Over half our marriages had a duration of five years or less.[10] A selectivity factor may apply to our study in this regard. Nullity focuses on the validity of consent to marriage and consequently it is normally easier to process an application relating to a marriage of short duration. Therefore, couples who have stayed together for long periods are less likely to proceed with their recourse to the Tribunal and this may depress the average duration of the marriages in the present study.

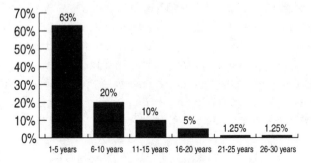

Figure 2.14 Duration of Marriage

In summary, the following groups were present in disproportionate numbers among the applications received by Galway
Tribunal in 1993: couples who were married during the period 1986
to 1990; couples who were separated for five years or under, and
couples whose marriages had a duration of five years or less.

Children

The couples in our sample had an average of 1.12 children. A very
large minority (41.2%) had no children while the highest family size
was five. When the childless couples are excluded, the average family size increased to 1.91. The marriages of the childless couples
endured for 4.12 years on average, while the total sample had an
average duration of marriage of 6.2 years. The female members of
the study ranged in age from twenty to fifty years at the time of separation; the average being 28.9 years. Therefore, few women had
passed child bearing age when separation occurred. In general, we
can conclude the presence of children is associated with longer
duration of marriage. It is likely that couples with children may
regard the perceived need of their children to have two cohabiting
parents as a disincentive to separate.

The interval from the birth of the couple's final child to their
separation varied considerably. In two cases, the couple separated
before the birth of their final child. The maximum interval was 22
years, while the average was 5 years. Due to the wide variation
involved, it was not possible to reach conclusions regarding the
association, if any, between the birth of children and the final separation. Figure 2.15 presents a breakdown of the number of children
per couple and substantially reflects O'Higgins' 1974 research. Her
study group had an average duration of marriage of 6.7 years, the
women being on average aged 29.4 when separation occurred.
However, the average number of children born to the couples in
O'Higgins' sample was greater by a factor of three (3.38 children).[11]
This reflects the overall drop in fertility within marriage which has
occurred in recent decades.

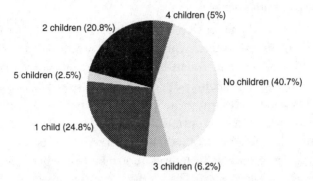

Figure 2.15 Number of Children per Couple

Recourse to counselling

Marital problems were not always the original focus of approaches made by members of our sample to counselling services. In several cases the counselling began by addressing other issues and then proceeded to address the marital difficulties and to involve the other partner. This pattern was most common among those receiving residential treatment for alcoholism. In this section, we shall include all counselling at which the couples' marital problems were discussed, irrespective of the original focus of the counselling.

Half of our subjects attended counselling at which their marital problems were discussed. Women were most likely to attend: the relevant figures are 57.3% for women and 42.5% for men. An indication that women were the principal proponents of counselling lies in the fact that only one husband attending counselling while his wife didn't do so. The reverse is true in 16.2% of cases. In 41.2% of couples both attended counselling, while in an equal percentage of cases neither party attended. On average the marriages of couples where both parties attended counselling endured 1.3 years longer than couples where only one or neither party attended. This divergence may be explained by the positive effect of counselling or by a selectivity factor, i.e. the couples more committed to the survival of their marriage may also be more likely to avail of counselling.

Subsequent relationships

The term second relationship is ambiguous. Its application can vary from a cohabiting couple who may have contracted a civil marriage, to a male-female friendship which may or may not develop into a long-term intimate relationship. The question of subsequent relationships is relevant to the Tribunal in that the granting of a decree of nullity may, if deemed necessary for pastoral reasons, be accompanied by a limitation on the right of one or both parties to re-marry. In compiling the figures quoted below, only relationships which are or were considered by the person involved as likely to endure long-term are included. Relationships which were never considered by the participant to be more than a fling are not included.

Among our sample, 67.5% of members became involved in another relationship after the break-up of his/her marriage. Men were more likely than women to form a subsequent relationship: the relevant figures are 70% and 65% respectively. In 87.5% of marriages at least one partner formed a new relationship, while in 42.7% of cases, both partners did so. Male petitioners were the group most likely to form a second relationship (77.4%), while the equivalent figure for female petitioners was 62.5%. These findings contrast with O'Higgins research in 1974. She reports that of the forty women in her study, one was cohabiting and three others had a male friend.[12] This contrast constitutes further evidence of a less restrictive attitude towards sexual involvement in Ireland.

CONCLUSION

The information presented above indicates that our subjects married partners who resemble themselves in geographic origin, social class, educational standard, religion, ethnic group, nationality and age. Even those who met their future spouse abroad rarely ventured far beyond his/her own ethnic, religious and social group. The homogeneity between the partners in the marriages studied is the most striking aspect of their social profile. This finding is not entirely surprising given that the tendency to marry within one's own group is present in most societies.

The gender imbalance between the petitioners is largely

counter-balanced by the high level of participation by respondents. The growing trend among Irish couples to become sexually active prior to marriage is reflected in our study. The fact that the more recent marriages display higher levels of sexual involvement supports the view that this trend is increasing. The level of religious practice in our subjects is somewhat lower than the high rate that characterises the wider Irish population. Our couples were younger than average at the time of marriage. The national trend for brides to be younger than their husbands is reflected in the sample. We also found that premarital pregnancy coincided with shorter courtships and earlier marriages. While duration of courtship varied greatly, our findings reflect those of Murphy's Galway-based study.

Most couples who applied to the tribunal in 1993 had very brief marriages and had separated within the previous three years. Our findings reflect O'Higgins' 1974 study in terms of the average duration of the marriage. However a significant change is evident in the three-fold drop in the average number of children per couple. A very large minority of couples in our study had no children. The interval from the birth of the couple's last child to their separation varied greatly and did not appear to indicate any significant association between child-birth and the timing of separation. About half our subjects attended counselling, with women being most likely to avail of this service. Attendance at counselling by both partners coincided with longer duration of marriage. Two in three participants were involved in new relationships. Evidence of a more liberal approach to sexual involvement was detected in the contrast with O'Higgins' 1974 findings regarding this point.

CHAPTER THREE

The Path Towards Marriage

The Irish family has evolved from being primarily an impersonal institution to a more supportive environment in which the emotional and personal needs of the participants are met. The emphasis has shifted from adherence to authority to personal choice. This change is especially evident in the case of marriage. People choose their own partners, decide the basis of the relationship, determine if the relationship meets their needs, and remain or depart accordingly. This has led to a change from a relatively homogeneous body of sexual relationships to a more diversified reality.

In previous decades, people in rural Ireland effectively had four choices: marriage for those who could secure an economic livelihood, religious life, non-married life as an assisting relative on a sibling's farm, or emigration. The development of industry and changes in social attitudes led to an explosion of choice. The selection of a spouse ceased to be the ordered process that it had been in the past when economic exigencies and patriarchal control were the dominant factors. Instead, personal preference became the key factor in deciding the 'who', 'when' and 'if' of marriage.

In this chapter, we shall review the life experiences of our subjects prior to marriage. This will include a consideration of how they actually choose their marriage partners. Many commentators speak of the increasing individualisation of Irish society. Spousal selection is a particular manifestation of this trend. Previously, the only socially acceptable form of sexual relationship was marriage as described by authors such as Arensberg and Kimball. In the current understanding of marriage, individuals now have personal control over the choice of marital partner, the nature of their premarital relationship and whether or not to marry, remain married or to leave and form a new relationship. The impersonal system of marrying a person with little or no prior personal contact has given way to an extensive process of courtship that frequently includes sexual involvement and cohabitation. Despite today's emphasis on individual preference, people do not live in a cultural vacuum. Society continues to encourage certain types of behaviour and discourage others. In this chapter, we shall look at the interaction between social norms and individual freedom in the area of marriage.

The records of the Galway Regional Marriage Tribunal contain detailed replies from the principal parties and from the witnesses regarding their experience of life prior to marriage. Points covered in the tribunal files include the parties' home backgrounds, education and work records, pressures towards marriage or advice against marriage and their concept of marriage. The parties are also asked to comment on previous relationships and the reason for their termination. This information allows us to construct and analyse our subjects' beliefs, experiences and expectations in relation to marriage.

DYSFUNCTIONAL FAMILIES OF ORIGIN

It is frequently argued that an association exists between the model of married and family life experienced by a person in his/her family of origin and his/her understanding of marriage as an adult.[1] The tribunal records include comments from the parties, from their witnesses and occasionally from psychologists or other professionals, regarding the family of origin of our subjects. In 60% of the marriages in our sample at least one party described his/her home background as unhappy and as constituting a negative influence on his/her future life. Virtually equal numbers of men and women regarded their home background negatively.

The concept of 'dysfunctional family of origin' is equivocal and consequently detailed statistical analysis is difficult. However, it is possible to identify particular factors in families of origin which had a negative impact on the person's ability to live out married life. The issues which we have identified are marital problems

Issue*	Percentage	Number of Marriages
Dysfunctional family of origin - men	36.25%	29
Dysfunctional family of origin - women	35%	28
Marital problems - parents	25%	20
Alcohol abuse	21.25%	17
Infidelity	12.50%	10
Excessive strictness	7.50%	6
Child sexual abuse	7.50%	6
Death of a parent	5%	4
Adoption	3.75%	3
Absence of tangible affection	Data does not permit calculation	
Conflict between parents and child	Data does not permit calculation	

* *The family of origin of each person may be characterised by more than one problem issue.*

Table 3.1 Issues in Family of Origin

between parents, alcohol abuse by parents, infidelity, excessive strictness, child sexual abuse, death of a parent, adoption, the absence of tangible affection and a conflictive relationship between parent and child. Table 3.1 summarises the number of cases involved in each area.

Marital problems experienced by parents

Twenty members of our study referred to serious problems in their parents' marriage. In all cases, these problems are regarded by the person concerned as constituting a major problem in his/her life and as relevant to the breakdown of the marriage. In thirteen cases, despite the existence of problems in their marriage, the parents continued to share the same house, while seven couples separated. There is no clear delineation between situations where parents, despite the breakdown of their marriage, continued to share the family home and cases where they separated. In all cases, the subjects believed that their parent's marital problems had a detrimental effect on their own ability to find happiness in marriage. No participant in the study expressed a view as to whether it would have been less traumatic if their parents had continued living together or had separated.

Quotations from individual cases serve to illustrate the impact of parental marital disharmony on the children in later life. A female stated that, 'My father and mother ... were on the point of breaking up. Life was very stressful for us ... I grew up with complexes ... I totally lacked confidence as a result of my upbringing.' Speaking of her husband, another woman remarked: 'From his family background, I understood why he dominated me so much. He wasn't going to let the situation arise like when his mother had dominated his father, thus he dominated me.'

Our study supports the view that marital problems in the family of origin are very traumatic for the children concerned. The evidence indicates that the effect was far reaching and extended into adult life and impacted negatively on their own marriages.

Death of a parent

In four cases, a parent of a participant died during his/her childhood. In two cases, the family was socially deprived and after the death of the husband, the mother found it impossible to impose discipline on her teenage children. Several teenage members of both families became involved in drink, drugs and brawling. They left school early and at best secured intermittent, unskilled employment and several experienced broken marriages. In all cases, the contributors to the files believe that the death of a parent had a detrimental effect on personal development and later ability to live out married life. However, the sample is too small to permit general conclusions.

Absence of tangible affection

A poor relationship between parents and children is the most frequently cited problem in this section. In some cases no tangible problem, such as violence, alcoholism or material deprivation, was present yet the person concerned regarded his/her childhood as unhappy.

Occasionally the lack of tangible affection arose from the parents' excessive work commitments. In one such case, a witness remarked:

They spoiled him with material things, but he really hungered for love ... he had tremendous freedom, but he would have preferred his parents to notice him and to set down guidelines.

Such children were frequently cared for by an employee or a relative while the parents immersed themselves in business. In other cases, the hectic social life of the parents resulted in the children being unsupervised for long periods. In cases involving the lack of tangible affection between parents and children, the effect is frequently summarised in the following terms: 'He did not receive love as a child and, therefore, he could not give love as an adult.'

Our study indicates that the lack of a close affective bond between parents and children is detrimental to the children's subsequent ability to cope with intimate relationships, particularly marriage, in adult life.

Excessive strictness

Excessive strictness is depicted as a major factor in the childhood of six individuals. This included a strict disciplinary regime, often incorporating extensive use of corporal punishment. The discipline often prevented the children from engaging in normal social contact.

A strict home regime often impacted on the decision to marry. Some married to escape a harsh home, while others married under pressure from their parents against their own better judgement. One family pushed their daughter to marry a man from a family which they saw as socially desirable. A witness stated, 'Even though she was distinctly uncomfortable with the idea [of marriage] … [her] family were taken by the standing of the [other] family.'

Marriage as an escape is evident in this quotation from a witness: 'She … went ahead with the marriage as a kind of escape from home. It was her first romance.'

Excessive discipline frequently impeded normal social interaction in childhood and affected the young person's social development. A strict domestic regime was often associated with the lack of close child-parent bonds. This shortcoming in childhood inhibited the development of skills required to cope with intimate adult relationships. In all cases where an excessively strict home situation existed, it is seen as being relevant to the person entering into an ill-advised marriage. The decision to marry was often made without sufficient thought, due either to a desire to escape parental pressure or to a lack of parental support or meaningful advice.

Conflict between parents and children

Problems in childhood were often more tangible. In some cases, there is reference to an aggressive relationship between parents and children. Such relationships were characterised by verbal or physical violence.

Difficulties in the relationship between mother and daughter were regarded by witnesses as particularly significant. Women from such homes state that they grew up with low self-esteem. In violent homes the children frequently lived in fear. One left home while still in his mid-teens. A psychiatrist describes him as suffering from a personality disorder and regards his home background as a contributing factor. Pressure to achieve academically was a factor in some cases.

Our study indicates that a discordant relationship between parents and children has negative consequences in adult life. The desire to leave an unhappy home reduced the level of discretion being exercised in the selection of a marriage partner. The lack of a close affective bond with parents disrupted the normal socialisation process and inhibited the development of skill needed to engage in adult intimate relationships such as marriage.

Alcohol abuse

Seventeen members of our study regard alcohol abuse by a parent as disruptive of their childhood. Alcohol abuse was frequently linked with violence, infidelity and marital problems among the parents.

Excessive drinking by the mother had the greatest impact on the children. In one case, the mother's drinking resulted in a neighbouring couple assuming almost complete responsibility for the child. In another case, a witness links alcohol abuse in the family of origin to the martial problems experienced by the children. She remarked: 'Nothing but drink ... and continuous rows. There was never any stability in the family ... [almost all] the marriages in that house have broken up.' Another witness described an alcoholic husband as 'inheriting' the problem from his parents, both of whom drank excessively.

Alcohol abuse by a parent is depicted as being severely disruptive of socialisation. It is associated with several other problems, all of which further disrupted the children's formative years. Its consequences included the destruction of a positive model of home life and the impairment of the children's ability to live out marriage in later life.

Infidelity by a parent

Infidelity by a parent occurred during the childhood of ten subjects. Mothers and fathers were unfaithful in equal numbers. Parental infidelity is depicted in the Tribunal files as having a detrimental influence on the children's personal development, on their understanding of marriage and on their ability to succeed in marriage. One witness remarked: 'Her parents would have gone out with other people while ... [she] was growing up. [She saw] no problem with [infidelity] when she got married.'

In three cases, witnesses make an explicit link between a parent having an extramarital affair and the child subsequently being unfaithful in marriage. The witnesses regard infidelity on the part of the mother as having a greater impact on the children than infidelity by the father.

Child sexual abuse

Child sexual abuse was experienced by six participants in the study: five female, one male. In all cases the alleged perpetrator was a family member and all the victims experienced sexual difficulties in marriage. Three females explicitly related their sexual difficulties in adult life to their childhood experiences. Comments include : 'I always felt unclean in that [sexual] area'; 'I always felt dirty'; and '[sex was] horrible for me'. A psychologist relates the personality disorders suffered by the male victim as an adult, to his childhood experiences. Due to the dynamics of child sexual abuse, it is probable that the actual number of people who were sexually abused in childhood is higher.[2] An association between the victims of child sexual abuse and later problems in adult intimate relationships is supported by this study.

Adoption

Three participants in our study were reared by adoptive parents. One did not co-operate with the tribunal and we have little information on the impact adoption had on him. Another was adopted by an elderly couple and a close parental bond did not develop. In the final case, despite the development of a close bond with the adoptive parents, the child became unruly as a teenager and marriage was occasioned by pregnancy. In all three cases, no association is posited between adoption and difficulties in marriage. The person's feelings regarding adoption are not explored in detail and therefore conclusions are not possible.

The impact of adoption on personal development, and particularly the ability to succeed in marriage, is an area where more research is required. Our sub-sample is too small and the data too meagre to permit even provisional conclusions. It is likely that the association, if any, between adoption and problems in marriage is complex and may be closely related with the person's self-image.

Conclusion

An unhappy home background impacts on marriage in two ways. Marriage may be entered into prematurely as a strategy to escape from the unhappy home situation. Even where the desire to 'escape' does not of itself propel the person into an ill-advised marriage, it can serve to compound the effect of other pressures. Fear of a parent's reaction is frequently mentioned by participants in our study as adding to the pressure created by a premarital pregnancy. Secondly, an unhappy home background contributed to the reduction of our subjects' ability to live out a marital relationship. Some cases contain professional psychological evidence in support of this point. Our study supports the thesis that the model of marriage witnessed in the family of origin is likely to be the model which he/she will carry into adult life. While a simple 'inheritance' theory is insufficient, it is clear from our study that marital problems do cross generations.

SOCIAL AND EDUCATIONAL FACTORS

In chapter two, we saw a pronounced homogeneity between the partners to the marriages in our study regarding educational attainment and social background. Therefore, it is not surprising that these factors were significant in the relationships of only three couples.

The social and educational homogeneity between our couples ensured that such distinctions were not major features of their relationships. In the small number of relationships where these factors were present, they were not regarded as being of decisive importance. Factors such as the partners' ability to relate on a personal level are depicted as being of greater importance. In all cases, the parties and the witnesses regard educational and social differences as relatively minor in the hierarchy of factors which were predictive of the failure of the unions concerned.

PREVIOUS RELATIONSHIPS

The level of detail regarding previous relationships in the tribunal files varies considerably. In most cases, the existence of a previous relationship, its importance in the life of the participant, its duration, and the reason for its termination, are noted. Relationships which are perceived to have had a significant impact on the decision to marry and the person's ability to live out marriage are described in greater detail. In many cases the experience of previous relationships is regarded as having contributed to the maturing process of the individual. However, in a minority of instances a previous relationship is depicted as having a negative impact on the marriage. Table 3.2 summarises the frequency with which certain issues arising from previous relationships occurred in our sample.

Issue	Percentage	Number of cases
Previously married	3.75%	3
Presence of a child	8.75%	7
Insignificant previous relationships		Almost all participants
Significant previous relationships		Data does not permit calculation

Table 3.2 Issues Arising From Previous Relationships

Insignificant previous relationships

Several premarital relationships were in the nature of teenage romances. Frequently, such relationships are depicted as contributing to the maturing of the participants. A woman stated: 'I went with a fellow for a while ... it fizzled out. I was fifteen.' A man stated: 'I went out with a girl for one year, but when I found that she was getting too serious about our relationship, I broke it off.' Relationships ended for various reasons including emigration by one or other party, disapproval by a parent, and meeting another girl or boy. In all these cases, the common thread is the non-serious nature of the relationships and they are not depicted as having a negative impact on the participants or the marriage.

Other relationships ended for more traumatic reasons such as violence or, in one case, 'he was into drugs'. Some participants did not regard these relationships as significant. It is reasonable to postulate that some relationships had a greater impact on the participants and their marriages, than was realised by the participants or recorded in the tribunal files. This lack of perception may have been relevant to the problems in their future marriages.

The presence of a child from a previous relationship

One of the most tangible ways in which a previous relationship impacted on a marriage was the female party having responsibility for a child conceived during the relationship. No males in the study had responsibility for, or referred to the existence of, a child from a previous relationship. Seven women (8.75%) had this responsibility. The relationship with the father was frequently short lived and ended before or shortly after the birth of the child. One mother stated:

> The father of my child ... wanted to go [abroad] ... He was gone when I realised that I was pregnant. To this day, he may not know of the baby.

The presence of a child impacted on the mothers and their marriages in various ways. In two cases, the male party's parents opposed the marriage on the grounds that the woman had a child by another man. In some cases, the presence of the child created tensions in the marriage. One man states: 'I wasn't ready to take on the responsibility of her child.'

In three cases, witnesses believe that the fact that the woman had a child impaired her discretion in selecting a marriage partner. In one case a witness stated: 'Since she had a child, she might have felt that she would have found it difficult to find a husband and when [he] did propose marriage, she ... felt that this was her only chance.'

In some cases, the witnesses believe that having responsibility for a child had a maturing effect on the mother. In reply to the question 'Did you regard the husband/wife as mature ... at the time of marriage?', a witness responds that 'she had to be because of [the child].' However, in the same case the man regards the presence of the child as mitigating against the success of the marriage.

In conclusion, we can say that the presence of a child from a previous relationship impacted significantly on the mother's decision to marry by impairing her discretion in selecting a husband. There is evidence of prejudice against a woman, who had a child from a previous relationship, as a partner in marriage. This attitude is frequently expressed by the husband's parents. The women concerned appeared to be aware of this prejudice and accepted that they were unlikely to have a wide choice of potential marriage partners. However, the husbands did not appear to reflect this prejudice. In only two cases is there evidence that the presence of the child from a previous relationship was a significant factor in the breakdown of the marriage.

Significant previous relationships

The ending of a relationship was often traumatic and occasionally a sense of attachment to a previous girl/boy friend remained. A woman stated that her parents would not permit her to marry the person that she loved. 'No one would listen to what I had to say ... I had no feelings for [my future husband].' A witness expressed the view that 'she should have run away with the first fellow'.

Some subjects conducted parallel relationships prior to marriage. A witness remarked:

[He] had been going out with a girl for four or five years ... They used have rows over her and when that happened, [he] would go back to [the previous girl]. He could always hold her as a threat over [his future wife].

In some cases, the problems in the courtship or subsequent marriage had been present in a previous relationship. These usually centred on alcohol abuse, violence, financial irresponsibility or infidelity. In one case, the male party had been unfaithful to his previous girlfriend and to his wife before and during the marriage. Another man was violent towards both his previous girlfriend and his future wife. In both cases the decision to marry was made in the context of an unplanned pregnancy.

The impact of a significant previous relationship is evident in the area of discretion before marriage and the person's subsequent commitment to the marriage. The uncertainty regarding which relationship to pursue served to dilute the person's commitment to the courtship and subsequent marriage. Discretion and commitment became diminished and the marriage was subject to an enhanced risk of failure.

Previously married

There are no examples in our study of people who had been previously married and whose marriage had been annulled or otherwise dissolved. However, three participants had been widowed. In one case a widower and widow married, while in another a widower married a much younger woman.

Expectations of marriage among those who were married previously varied considerably. In one case, the man had been the dominant party in his first marriage and sought to carry this model into the new marriage. The female was more assertive than his previous wife. She stated: 'I was taken for granted ... we got married very quickly ... if we hadn't, I would have gotten to know him a lot better and ... the marriage would not have taken place.'

All three participants presumed that the second marriage would bring them happiness, just as the first had. They carried a ready-made model of marriage into the new situation and found it difficult to make the necessary adjustments to accommodate the needs and wishes of their new partner.

Conclusion

Previous relationships played an important role in the development of expectations of marriage and impacted on maturity and
discretion. The freedom to form or terminate relationships has led
to a considerable variation in the nature and duration of such associations. Consequently many relationships do not result in marriage. Most previous relationships had little if any negative impact
on the marriage. Many had a positive impact and the interaction
involved served to progress the development of skills appropriate
to intimate relationships. However, a minority of previous relationships had a negative impact.

PRESSURES TOWARDS MARRIAGE

In several cases, the decision-making process concerning marriage
was not entirely free. Pressures ranged from pregnancy or a desire
to escape an unhappy home background, to a belief that the proposed marriage constituted the person's only opportunity to marry.
The impact of an unhappy home background has been explored
above. In this section we shall look at the impact of an unplanned
pregnancy or birth on the decision to marry. Table 3.3 presents the
number of cases involving each factor.

Pressure	Percentage	Number of cases
Dysfunctional family of origin	60%	48
Pregnancy	33.75%	27
Birth prior to marriage	11.25%	9
Sundry	Data does not permit calculation	

Table 3.3 Pressures Towards Marriage

Pregnancy at time of marriage

Premarital pregnancy *per se* was not always a pressure towards
marriage. One woman stated: 'There was no pressure on us to enter
marriage, not even from the fact that I was pregnant. We planned to
marry [that year] anyway.' However, unplanned pregnancy in tan-
dem with family coercion was the most common pressure towards
marriage in our sample.

Sexual activity outside marriage was not always accompanied by a parallel development in the ability of the participants to deal with the consequences. Elements of the old and new approaches co-existed. The people who conducted sexually active, though frequently superficial, relationships felt obliged to marry if pregnancy occurred. Alcohol was frequently associated with the pregnancy. One man stated: 'Drink had a lot to do with [my girlfriend] becoming pregnant.'

Some cases contained an openness to options other than marriage. In the following mid-1980s marriage, the woman had preferred to postpone consideration of marriage until after the birth. She stated:

I wasn't in control ... If my mother had not reacted in such an extreme manner, I wouldn't have married ... I was in favour of us waiting until after the child was born ... If we had waited ... we wouldn't ever have married. ... The priest asked us if we were getting married of our own accord, we assured him that we were.

A generational difference is apparent here. The mother saw marriage as the only course of action, while her daughter was open to other options. However, her traditional respect for her mother determined the outcome. The evolving nature of attitudes towards pregnancy outside of marriage is apparent.

There are few references to contraception in our cases. Some couples simply state that they took precautions. Others state that they did not consider the possibility of pregnancy and 'simply hoped it wouldn't occur'. There are occasional references to the restricted availability of contraception in Ireland prior to the mid-1980s. However, availability was not always the key issue. Despite living abroad and the woman's mother urging her to 'be careful', one woman still had an unplanned pregnancy.[3]

There is evidence that the nature of the pressure exerted by a pre-marriage pregnancy has evolved over recent decades. The following quotations illustrate this point. A woman who became pregnant before marriage in the 1960s describes how she and her boyfriend felt obliged to leave the country. 'We eloped ... I had to get married to keep my baby … there was no question of staying single and living together and having the baby.'

Ten years later, a couple in similar circumstances still felt compelled to marry, but remained in their home area. The woman stated:

> It was only when I discovered that I was pregnant that I wanted to get married. I thought that if I didn't, my father would put me out of the house. I told none of my family I was pregnant until after I was married.

The following case shows how the situation had evolved further in the 1980s. The male party stated:

> But for the [pregnancy] we could have just as easily broken up as become married … I felt that we had to get married … My mother had strong Catholic beliefs … I didn't want to disappoint her. My father took it more in his stride. [Her] mother was different.

The pressure to marry in this case is indirect and consists in a desire not to disappoint a parent, rather than actual coercion. It is notable that only one parent had strong views on the necessity of marriage. The lack of a focus on the relationship is also apparent.

The impact of a premarital pregnancy lies primarily in the area of decision-making. In most cases marriage was not seriously considered until the pregnancy was discovered. The focus of the decision moved from issues regarding the couple's future life to a solution to the problems created by the pregnancy. These problems centred on a sense of shame and a feeling the couple had let down their families. Though this pressure was not always explicit, it was real for the couple concerned. In some cases, the option of postponing the marriage until after the birth was explored. Direct intervention by the families frequently excluded that option.

Birth prior to marriage

In nine cases (11.25%) marriage took place after the birth of a child to the couple. Their parents played a proactive role in encouraging most of these couples to marry. Seven of these couples cohabited before marriage. One woman was thrown out by her parents when they became aware that she was pregnant; the couple then began to live together. Her mother had previously advised her to use contraception. Another female states: 'I wanted to be with [my future husband] so I had to get married because my parents would not allow me to live with him.'

Social and parental pressure were key elements in encouraging couples who had previously given birth to a child to marry. Most such couples had cohabited and several were experiencing problems in their relationships. However, the pressures experienced by pregnant brides were reflected in the experience of these couples. The focus shifted from the couples' relationship and future to avoiding embarrassment or the loss of the child.

Other pressures

Some participants cited other factors as limitations on the exercise of their discretion regarding marriage. A woman spoke of how the other party used to, 'threaten to kill himself. It was emotional blackmail … I was afraid I might be responsible if he did harm himself. I was too young to be able to take a stand against something like that.'

Another woman referred to her desire to be married by a certain age as a factor in her ill-advised decision to marry. A man cited the length of the courtship, his partner's ill health and public reaction as pressures towards marriage. He stated:

> I was concerned about what people thought. They were talking in terms of me having wasted all these years of a girl's life and blackguarding her … I had some sense that it was my vocation to marry [her] and look after her … I was conscious of her illness.

The severity of the pressure involved and the ability of the other partner to cope are the relevant factors here. Frequently, such cases exposed considerable limitations in both parties. Marriages originating in such circumstances had extremely inauspicious beginnings.

Conclusion

We have discussed several factors which served to restrict freedom of choice regarding marriage. A key factor was the individual's ability to cope with the pressure involved. The pressure usually centred on a fear of loss of reputation within the local community and on the alienation of the affection of parents or family. The focus shifted from a decision regarding marriage *per se* to the adoption of a tactic to resolve a crisis.

A conflict between old and new approaches to sexuality and relationships emerges from this section. The couples concerned saw an active sexual relationship as appropriate in their situation. However, many lacked the ability to avoid or cope with a possible consequence of their behaviour, pregnancy. Pregnancy brought inherited values and norms into play and marriage and spousal selection ceased to be matters of individual choice. Most couples seemed to occupy an intermediate stage between traditional and modern. The modern is evident in terms of the freedom to pursue relationships on the basis of individual preferences. The traditional emerges in the role played by familial and social pressures in effecting marriage.

The normal process of the selection of a partner for marriage was disrupted by external pressures for the couples in this section. In many relationships, there was no decision regarding, or in some cases even mention of, marriage prior to the pressure coming into play. The impact of the most common source of pressure, premarital pregnancy, is greatest in the case of the woman; she is literally left holding the baby or faced with unpalatable options such as adoption or abortion. The opportunity to exercise discretion is removed and dysfunctional relationships become marriages. The couple lose control of events and marry on the basis of a partner or relationship which, in other circumstances, they would reject as inappropriate to marriage.

NATURE OF THE COURTSHIP

In societies where marriage is based on personal choice, courtship is a central part of the process of selecting a marriage partner. The premarital relationship is a key part of preparation for marriage during which the couple seek to develop a close inter-personal relationship. In this section, we shall review the courtships experienced by our subjects and identify the factors which were predictive of marriage breakdown. We shall look at courtship under four headings: superficial attraction; the nature of decision regarding marriage; specific problems in courtship; and cohabitation prior to marriage. Due to the ill-defined nature of these categories it is not possible to calculate the specific number of cases under each heading.

Superficial attraction

Almost all couples state that the initial attraction was superficial, e.g. the other person's physical attractiveness or vibrant personality. Under normal circumstances, the initial superficial attraction matures into a more solidly based relationship. However, the distinctive feature of most of our cases was that this progression did not occur.

Our data contains numerous illustrations of the superficial nature of many premarital relationships. These comments by a witness are commonplace: 'What attracted her was his appearance and that he was driving a flashy car – no common interests. They liked fighting and did so any chance that they got.'

Many cases involved the lack of a conscious decision regarding marriage. The term drift is usually employed in such cases. The following example is typical: 'It was just an infatuation that would soon disappear altogether.'

In many cases the sexual aspect of the relationship was accorded a disproportionate importance, and physical intimacy was not matched by emotional intimacy. One woman stated: 'Our relationship was very physical. It wasn't really a relationship. A huge part of my huge love for him was physical attraction and physical desire … it was more a sexual need.'

The common thread in the cases cited above is the lack of a deep foundation to the relationship. They resemble teenage infatuations rather than relationships appropriate to couples who are about to make an exclusive, permanent commitment to each other. There is evidence of a lack of a deliberative decision regarding marriage. Physical intimacy was not accompanied by shared meaning or definition of roles.

Decision regarding marriage

In almost all cases, at least one party states that he/she entered marriage without giving it the necessary consideration. Even in cases where obvious complications such as an unwanted pregnancy are not present, there is evidence of couples drifting towards marriage rather than actually deciding to marry.

A feature of superficial courtships is their group nature. Many couples, despite spending a lot of time together, did not relate on a deep level. A witness described such a courtship: 'He went to the pub about five nights and she would be with him … it all seemed lovey-dovey in those days. She followed him around and didn't ask any questions.'

In the same case, the wife stated 'a lot of our courtship was in groups … it seemed like a dream'. However, shortly into the marriage she discovered his drinking problem, which the witnesses state was obvious beforehand. A lack of communication was a feature of such courtships.

Such descriptions are commonplace in the tribunal records. Couples who lived together prior to marriage did not necessarily avoid this scenario. A witness made the following comment regarding a cohabiting couple:

> Their courtship was very childish. It was all about little romantic things … they were on their own little cloud. I'm not aware of they [sic] planning for future married life other than the type of curtains they would like.

The similarity with couples who, though sexually active, did not cohabit prior to marriage is striking.

The almost unconscious drifting towards marriage is illustrated by the man in the following case. He stated: 'We never became engaged … we drifted towards marriage rather than make any formal decision about it.'

Courtships conducted on a restricted basis, such as weekends, appear to be particularly prone to superficiality and drift. A comparison with a control group of couples who experienced happy marriages after weekend courtships would be helpful in this regard.

It is also notable that our subjects did not attach major significance to their engagement. Engagement is the final stage in courtship during which the couple make a public declaration of their intention to marry. The period of engagement provides the couple with an opportunity to engage in active consideration of all aspects of their future life together and a final opportunity to deepen their interpersonal bond. While all the couples in our sample became engaged prior to marriage, this frequently involved little more than the purchase of a ring to be worn by the woman. In many cases, especially where pressures such as premarital pregnancy led to a hasty marriage, the purchase of the ring took place shortly before the marriage. Even in cases where the period of engagement was extended, many couples did not avail of the opportunity that it afforded to plan jointly for their future or to develop their relationship. In most cases there was little perceptible distinction between the relationship pre- and post-engagement. Where a distinction existed, it was most likely to be on the physical level; in some cases engagement was accompanied by the commencement of a sexual relationship or of cohabitation.

A common feature of the cases considered in this section is the absence of a reflective process, proportionate to the commitment being undertaken. A superficial courtship generally led to marriage, even when the freedom of the individuals to choose or to reject marriage was not unduly limited by circumstances or by external agents. Such marriages involved the absence of a decision, rather than a mistaken or ill-informed option. These cases are examples of people exercising individual choice regarding spousal selection without adequate reflection.

Problems in courtship

In many cases, specific problems which were present in courtship re-surfaced in marriage. Such cases are often characterised by extraordinary optimism on the part of one party and a failure by the other to alter his/her behaviour.

Naïveté is evident in the approach taken by some women. Several believed that the problem would disappear on marriage.

One woman articulated this attitude: 'I hoped that I would change him ... I was afraid of being left on the shelf.' Denial was evident in another woman's attitude: 'I wasn't sure if I wanted to [marry]; his drinking and temper all flashed before me ... I thought that it was just wedding morning nerves.' An extraordinary level of optimism is evident in these comments.

Violent behaviour was a problem in some courtships. A victim of a violent premarital relationship cited the birth of a child and social and familial pressures as coercive factors towards marriage. The girlfriend of an unfaithful partner married for similar reasons. The tendency to believe promises that married life would be different is evident in the case of this pregnant bride: 'I stayed with him in spite of his lies and his not turning up for dates. I was immature and I believed the promises he would make to me.'

A lack of realism underlies the sentiments expressed above. The behaviour of some participants and the naive approach of their partners betrays a lack of understanding of marriage. Both the behaviour and the shallowness of the reaction are predictive of problems in marriage. The hope that the other person's behaviour would change after marriage proved to be ill founded. On the contrary, the problems frequently intensified rather than diminished. The lack of a well-grounded, reflective process of meaningful interaction between the couple is evident.

Cohabitation prior to marriage

Twenty-two couples (27.5%) cohabited before marriage. Of these, fifteen experienced a premarital pregnancy and, in seven cases, birth occurred prior to marriage. These couples were subject to particular pressures which we have considered above. In this section, we shall focus on the effect of cohabitation *per se*, on the couple's preparation for marriage.

A pattern of couples persevering towards marriage despite the presence of major problems in their relationship is evident. Couples who lived together were subject to many of the same pressures that we have encountered in the general study. Many entered marriage on the basis of extraordinary optimism. Couples who lived together abroad were subject to particular pressures such as isolation from family and friends and loneliness. Therefore, they were more likely to continue in unsatisfactory or even abusive relationships rather than face life alone. Frequently, parental disapproval of premarital cohabitation had the ironic effect of a dysfunctional relationship being upgraded into an unhappy marriage.

Many cohabiting couples engaged in little serious discussion or forward planning. Statements that the parties never discussed the question of children or finances prior to marriage are common-place. A woman who lived with her boyfriend for a year before marriage referred to the absence of 'deep conversation', while the man stated that they didn't discuss the issue of children, previous relationships or even marriage itself.

It is noteworthy that almost all the couples who lived together prior to marriage did so away from their home area. Two couples lived together in the home of the parents of one party; however, in both cases, the family concerned lived abroad. Two other couples lived in the family home of one or other; however they specify that they had separate rooms. Living away from the couple's area of origin and particularly outside Ireland, served to liberalise attitudes regarding cohabitation.

It is striking that the issues which complicated the relationships of our overall sample affected cohabiting couples in the same way. Superficial courtships, lack of communication, marriage despite advice to the contrary, susceptibility to pressures from family or pregnancy, and coercion by a partner, all manifest themselves among cohabiting couples. Cohabitation served to highlight several factors which subsequently proved to be disruptive of the marriage. Nonetheless, the marriages took place. The view that premarital cohabitation serves to enhance the courtship process is not supported by the present study.

Conclusion

In this section we reviewed various features of our subjects' courtships. These included superficiality, the lack of a deliberative decision regarding marriage, cohabitation, and specific problems such as violence, alcohol abuse or infidelity. The freedom to engage in a relationship of one's own choosing was evident in all cases. However, the corresponding capacity to make appropriate decisions was frequently lacking. The absence, in most cases, of an effective period of engagement emphasised the casual nature of the premarital relationship. There is little evidence of the development of a close interpersonal relationship involving satisfactory roles for both partners. This augured poorly for a marriage based on negotiation and compromise.

SEXUAL ASPECTS OF COURTSHIP

The tribunal asks the principal parties to comment on the sexual aspects of their relationship prior to marriage. Most simply state that they were sexually active and that they experienced it as a loving aspect of their relationship. Those who were not sexually involved state that fact and usually add that their relationship found physical expression in other ways. Cases involving sexual problems usually include more detailed comments. In this section, we shall analyse this information with reference to the couples' relationship and progress towards marriage. Table 3.4 summarises the data regarding the sexual aspects of courtship.

Issue	Percentage	Number of cases
Sexually involved	67.50%	54
Pregnancy	37.50%	30
Cohabitation	28.75%	23
Birth	11.25%	9
Birth by another partner	8.75%	7
Abortion	6.25%	5

Table 3.4 Sexual Aspects of Courtship

Premarital sexual involvement

In only one case is there reference to sexual problems *per se* prior to marriage. The woman concerned stated: 'I couldn't admit to myself that he might never arouse me ... I did think that when we got married ... [he] would arouse in me the feelings of love, that I thought was [*sic*] there.'

The male party presents a similar picture and states that there were extremely few physical manifestations of affection prior to marriage. Both parties refer to wider problems in the relationship, such as an inability to discuss feelings. However, sexual problems emerged as a major problem in their marriage.

The most common difficulties in premarital sexual relationships was a perceived pressure on the woman to be sexually involved and a lack of other expressions of affection. Many men appear to have insisted on a sexual relationship as a *sine qua non* for the continuation of the relationship. One woman stated: 'I went along with him in order to hold on to him. Having no experience of [sex] I felt as if I was a child ... Apart from intercourse, ours wasn't a very affectionate relationship.'

In some cases, pressure to be sexually active co-existed with other problems. One woman refers to her partner's irresponsible attitude regarding pregnancy and his fear of ridicule regarding a public display of affection:

I didn't feel happy about it ... it was out of my control ... He'd keep at me physically ... I'd be worried about becoming pregnant ... he'd say 'that's up to you, what do you expect me to do about it?' ... He would hold hands if we were [away] but he wouldn't if we were [at home] in case someone he knew might see him.

An inconsistency between physical intimacy and the absence of emotional intimacy is apparent.

Even when sexual involvement was freely chosen, the experience was not always satisfactory from the woman's viewpoint. The male party was frequently unaware of her dissatisfaction. The only problem that men refer to, regarding the sexual relationship, concerned its perceived infrequency. As the next quotation illustrates, women often had a different perspective: 'It was only sex for the sake of sex ... there was never any kissing or cuddling ... we never really discussed it.'

In contrast with the general trend, in two relationships the woman wished for a more active sexual life. One man who cohabited with his girlfriend stated: '[She] wanted more of it and I didn't. I was too tired after work.'

An over concentration on the sexual served to obscure problems in the couple's overall relationship.

In almost all cases the woman was the dissatisfied partner. Most men appear to have been unaware of their partners' dissatisfaction. The key issues were pressure to be sexually active and a lack of emotional satisfaction. In speaking to a Church Tribunal, some women motivated by a desire to present themselves as morally virtuous, may have overstated the pressure on them to become sexually involved. However, it is reasonable to assume that many of these accounts are authentic. The desire of women to express and receive affection in physical manifestations other than sexual intercourse is also noteworthy. A female-male duality of approach is detectable. In crude terms, a female focus on quality can be contrasted with a male focus on quantity.

The problems in the pre-marriage sexual relationship were not primarily sexual, but related to the overall quality of the relationship. Problems in communication were most apparent. A distinction between sexual intimacy and emotional intimacy is manifest. The male party was frequently unaware of his partners' true feelings regarding a significant aspect of their relationship. Conversely, the female party was unable to communicate her true feelings to him. The lack of true intimacy is indicative of a shallow courtship and predictive of problems in marriage.

Moral considerations

Moral reservations regarding premarital sexual intimacy receive scant mention in the tribunal files. Dissatisfaction with the premarital sexual relationship is couched in emotional rather than moral terms. There are however a small number of references to moral considerations. One man states that his partner 'went through agonies of guilt about sexual intimacy'. A woman stated: '[He] would have pushed for sexual intimacy. I wouldn't have been happy about being so involved pre-marriage.'

In another case, the woman recalled that they were not 'sexually involved prior to marriage. I didn't wish to be and I didn't wish to become pregnant, partially out of respect for my parents.'

It is noteworthy that all references to moral considerations are made by women. This decline in the attachment of a moral dimension to premarital sexual intimacy supports the view that there has been a virtual revolution in the Irish approach to sexuality in recent decades. In some relationships, the woman's desire to continue the relationship gave the man the dominant position. Some women refer to consenting to behaviour that they had objections to, usually premarital sexual involvement, to ensure the continuation of the relationship.

Abortion

Four cases contain mention of premarital abortions. The references vary from cursory to more detailed comment. The sensitivity of the subject is reflected in the fact that in only one case is there a comment from a witness.

The size of our sub-sample precludes conclusions regarding the impact of abortion on courtship or marriage. In our limited sample, the impact on the individuals involved varied considerably. The emotional impact appears to be greatest in the case of women. However, while some women depict it as a gruesome experience others describe it in less traumatic terms. Some women do not refer to the abortion at all. This may relate to a desire to avoid embarrassment when speaking to a Church Tribunal or to a general preference not to discuss the issue. Some men were more supportive of their partners than others. Some present the abortion in detached terms, while others appear more sensitive.

Abortion is presented in most cases as an alternative to marriage. There are no references to abortion *per se* representing a major problem in the courtship or subsequent marriage or impeding the level of discretion exercised by either party. Abortion emerged on the borders of acceptable individual choice and it continues to be couched in terms which hint at moral unacceptability. It is regarded in very different terms to issues such as premarital sexual involvement or cohabitation. However, the fact that our sample is composed of applicants to a Church Tribunal may serve to emphasise the moral dimension of this issue.

Conclusion

An active sexual relationship is increasingly becoming a standard part of the premarital experience. A picture emerges of interaction between most couples resulting in both parties seeing a sexual relationship as appropriate and not involving feelings of guilt. Cohabitation is not universally acceptable, at least not in the couple's home area. Abortion continues to carry moral overtones.

Sexual problems *per se* are rarely mentioned in our cases. However, problems in the sexual sphere frequently reflected problems in other areas of the couple's relationship. A lack of effective communication was one such problem. Frequently, one partner was unaware of the other's dissatisfaction with aspects of their sexual relationship. For women, the most common causes of dissatisfaction were a perceived pressure to be sexually active and a lack of emotional fulfilment. Reflecting a traditional stereotype, infrequency was the principal problem identified by men. A lack of emotional intimacy and an inability to discuss key aspects of the relationship, emerge as the principal theme of this section.

CONTRACTUAL ASPECTS OF MARRIAGE

The Catholic Church regards marriage as a permanent, exclusive commitment that is open to children. If a person marries with the intention of excluding any of these elements, the resultant contract is invalid. All candidates for marriage are asked as part of the pre-nuptial enquiry process to affirm their acceptance of these elements. The tribunal asks both parties if, at the time of marriage, they consented to marriage in these terms. The recorded replies are generally short. Most give very brief affirmative responses and add that they presume that their partner saw marriage in a similar way.

All participants stated that they had intended to be faithful in marriage. However, in cases where infidelity was a problem in the marriage, the aggrieved party sometimes cast doubt on the unfaithful party's intentions regarding fidelity or his/her ability to be faithful. The following comment is typical:

> Perhaps on the day of the wedding she [intended to be faithful], but it went in one ear and out the other. I don't believe that she is

capable of being faithful. She was unfaithful before and during the marriage.

In many cases, there is evidence of a lack of reflection on the commitment to fidelity, rather than of a positive exclusion of such an undertaking.

A similar tendency is present regarding permanency. All the participants state that they were committed to a life-long marriage. Occasionally, they perceive their partner's commitment to permanency as qualified. The following comment is typical of many:

> He believed in marriage on his own terms. If he could drink and see other women and still have a wife at home to cook for him, then he would stay married for life.

There are no indications that our couples entered marriage conscious that separation was a readily available option. The evidence points to their understanding marriage as a permanent arrangement in a very casual way, rather than the influence of a 'divorce culture'.

Prior to marriage, couples were more likely to discuss the issue of children. Many agreed to postpone children until their financial situation was more secure.[4] However, the level of discussion regarding the impact that children would have on the marital relationship tended to be minimal. Discussion was limited to the optimal time to have the first child, and less frequently, the preferred number of children. In marriages involving pregnant brides, the couple usually stated that they had not reflected on the question of further children. A husband in such a case stated: 'We never discussed children ... [She] was pregnant and if things were okay financially, we would have welcomed other children.'

Though some couples entered marriage without reflecting on the question of children, all saw this issue as a legitimate object of their discretionary powers. The traditional attitude which viewed the number and timing of children as providential, has given way to an approach which sees these matters as discretionary.[5]

The grounds of intention against children, fidelity or permanence were not found to nullify any of the marriages in our study.[6] However, there is often scant evidence of a positive intention in their favour. The absence of reflection on these aspects of marriage is the most striking finding in this section. These aspects of marriage bring individual decision-making into contact with a pre-determined body of beliefs and commitments. Our subjects responded by overlooking, rather than rejecting, these commitments.

PRACTICAL PREPARATIONS

Some couples made little or no practical preparation for future married life. Hastily arranged marriages frequently took place with inadequate thought given to finances or accommodation. However, even in the absence of pressure to marry, a lack of practical preparation was a feature of some cases.

Couples who married in the context of an unplanned pregnancy frequently had made no practical preparations. A pregnant bride stated: 'We had no money saved. We hadn't arranged a place to live. My mother paid for the dresses.'

A similar recklessness is present in cases when there was no pressure to marry. A man stated: 'I didn't have a penny saved and I had no house ... [we] didn't have a clue as to what was involved in marriage.'

A lack of preparation went hand in hand with the absence of discussion. Several subjects entered marriage not knowing what his/her spouse earned. One woman stated: 'we discussed nothing ... I knew nothing about how much [he] earned but he always seemed to have lots of money.'

In some cases, there are indications that financial issues were seen as primarily a male responsibility. Some men stated: 'I had nothing saved'; 'I didn't have a house'. The following quotations also illustrate the point: 'He said he was going to buy a house'; and '[he] had already bought a house'. However, this attitude is held by a minority of couples. Most saw these issues as their joint responsibility.

The image of superficial premarital relationships is re-reinforced by the neglect of financial and accommodation issues. This neglect involved a lack of practical preparation. However, a lack of communication was also evident. A lack of discussion, irrespective of the level of preparation undertaken by one party independently of the other, augurs poorly for effective communication in marriage. A departure from the past is evident in that marriage was previously tied to secure economic prospects. In some cases in our sample, the neglect of these issues conveys an air of unreality.

FORMAL PREPARATION FOR MARRIAGE

All our couples had some formal preparation for marriage. Each person met the priest who officiated at the wedding and most attended, with 12-15 other couples, a four session pre-marriage course. A small number opted for a residential weekend course, which is more intensive in nature. Some couples had private meetings with a marriage counsellor. The latter group were usually referred by a priest, who felt that the proposed marriage was especially at risk. A small minority did not attend any formal preparation other than a meeting with a priest. This was usually due to an exceptional circumstance, such as the vehement opposition of the couple or logistical problems. The tribunal asks each person to comment on the formal preparation for marriage. Most offer brief comments, though some elaborate. In this section, we shall examine these comments and review the degree to which formal premarital preparation impacted on their relationship.

The general response to group pre-marriage courses was negative. Typical comments included 'it was no use', 'just fair', 'not great really'. Many doubted the relevance of the course to their needs: 'it didn't tell me anything that I did not already know; 'it wasn't for us, who were so long living together'; 'they didn't talk about anything that would make you understand anything any better' and 'a lot of it didn't apply to us as we were working and had a house'. Some objected to the compulsory aspect: 'We both went because we regarded it as compulsory' and '[He] looked on it as something we had to do'. Some criticised the presentation and format: 'The priest was great but the other people were getting embarrassed and didn't know how to put things. Also there were too many doing the course.'

Couples who undertook a residential pre-marriage course had similar reactions. One person stated: 'We went on an engaged weekend ... It was unbelievable; one couple broke down crying. The lead couple weren't on the planet.' The failure of the pre-marriage courses to challenge these couples is apparent.

Some participants focused on their own disposition. A pregnant bride stated: 'I was in shock'. One party felt that they 'were too young to understand', while another focused on immaturity: 'We were like two comedians at it.' A woman recalled that she 'was shy and embarrassed by it ... I remember him looking at me and getting me to laugh ... if I had listened, I might have learned from it.'

The husband of a pregnant bride states: 'We had our minds made up and we weren't going to be talked out of it by anyone.' The disposition of these participants is indicative of the formidable task involved in premarital preparation.

A small number of participants had positive comments. One described the course as 'good and interesting'. Another stated that the 'priest talked very straight. He warned us there could be tough times ahead'. A man described the counsellors who gave the course 'as great to listen to'. Another states: 'We found it to be interesting and good.' However, positive evaluations were few in number.

Women were more open to formal preparation for marriage than men. A woman 'found the course very good ... [but he] showed no interest and ruined it for me'. Several women attended all the sessions, while their partners missed some sessions. In some such cases the course proved beneficial. One woman stated:

> Only when confronted by the priest that we wouldn't get our papers if we didn't do something, did [he] actually attend. [Though he] wasn't happy with anything that had to do with priests ... he seemed to enjoy it and, at the end, we were closer as a couple.

There were some exceptions, where the man was positive and the woman negative. One man described it as 'very good', while his wife, somewhat ironically states: 'We could have done without it.' Cases where counselling succeeded, despite a hostile attitude towards the service, are extremely rare in our sample.

Conclusion

The comment of a participant regarding pre-marriage courses serve as a summary for this section. She stated:

I would tell couples the other side of what marriage is like and how hard it is to get out of marriage, rather than talk so much about money and budgeting. I would talk about personalities and how they effect each other. I would interview people as individuals and as couples, rather than have these open sessions where you can hide a lot.

The reaction to formal pre-marriage preparation indicates that it was not appropriate to the needs of most couples and that frequently couples were not open to counselling. The group format facilitated the desire of many participants to avoid playing an active part. Residential courses and individual meetings with priests or counsellors helped overcome the anonymity of the group situation. However, the disposition of the participants continued to be a decisive factor. Those under most pressure, or who had devoted least consideration to marriage, were frequently least receptive to counselling. Each subject met a priest prior to marriage. However, these meetings are rarely mentioned in the Tribunal files and are becoming perfunctory, as formal preparation for marriage increasingly becomes the reserve of specialist agencies. While there is scope for improving formal preparation for marriage, the current emphasis on individual autonomy will continue to make the task difficult.

CONCLUSION

Socialisation emerged as particularly important in our subject's premarital experience. In particular, the absence of a close affective bond between parents and child was depicted as predictive of problems in intimate relationships. A poor relationship with parents also contributed to some participants entering ill-advised marriages. The inability of some participants to seek the advice of parents at times of crisis mitigated against a well-considered decision regarding marriage.

Most previous relationships are depicted as positive and the interaction involved served to promote the maturing process in the participants. However, some impacted negatively on the parties. Some subjects retained an attachment to a previous partner and entered marriage with reduced commitment. The presence of a child from a previous relationship placed an additional responsibility on the couple as they entered marriage. Some were not equal to this responsibility. A disapprobation attached to women with a child from a previous relationship. This was manifest in parental opposition to their son's marriage to such a woman. Some unmarried mothers felt that the number of potential marriage partners available was restricted and were less discriminating in their willingness to become involved in relationships which could lead to marriage.

Sexual intimacy is seen by most members of the study as appropriate premarital behaviour. While this reflects the negotiation of roles within the relationship, it is likely that is also indicates a shift in identification. In the past, the church was the key reference group in determining sexual behaviour. While our data contains few explicit references to the role of peers or of the media, it is likely that our subjects regard their peers, and images transmitted through the media, as the key influences in this area. However, the persistent influence of parents and of the local community in relation to behaviour that carried a visible, public dimension, is also evident. Attitudes towards premarital pregnancy illustrates this point: couples who engaged in premarital sex were likely to feel compelled to marry if pregnancy occurred. The reason most frequently advanced for the necessity to marry in these circumstances, centres on on a wish not to disappoint parents, or a fear of a loss of reputation in the community. Parents and the local community were the key influences in making decisions on how to react to premarital pregnancy but they did not have the same relevance in the more private area of premarital sex. This pattern was also evident in the area of premarital cohabitation. Living together before marriage was largely restricted to couples living away from their home area. The couple were happy to live together but they did not wish their families of origin or home community to be aware of it.

Courtship is viewed in Irish society as an opportunity to build a close interpersonal relationship in anticipation of marriage. The cases reviewed above do not indicate that this process took place: superficiality is a constant theme. Interaction appears frequently to have been limited to areas such as the physical relationship and entertainment. Many couples did not even communicate effectively on basic matters such as finance or accommodation, and rarely reached the interpersonal relationship *per se* or their respective roles in marriage. This truncated interaction was often due to courtship being short-circuited into marriage by pregnancy or some other crisis. In other relationships, personal factors such as immaturity proved decisive. In all cases, the failure of the couple to interact effectively and become mutually significant others, was a significant handicap as they entered what should have been a negotiated, intimate relationship. The mechanisms to counteract shortcomings in courtship proved ineffective. Pre-marriage courses rarely served to alert the couples to the disquieting features inherent in their relationship. The negative disposition of the participants was a major obstacle. However, an increased focus on inter-personal aspects of marriage and the use of individual counselling, emerged as likely strategies to enhance formal pre-marriage preparation.

The contrast between the reality of the spousal selection in the Ireland of the 1930s and contemporary Ireland is more apparent than real. In the matchmaking system, the groom and bride were carefully matched in financial and social terms. They frequently married having had very little personal contact. There is also a remarkable homogeneity between the partners to our marriages, in social, educational, and even geographical terms. Most marriages in our study would have met the criteria of the old matchmaking system. Personal choice and contact with the other partner are hallmarks of the present system of mate-selection in Ireland. In most cases, this extends to sexual intimacy. However, it frequently does not encompass discussion of future married life and the details of their interpersonal relationship. Effectively, most of our couples entered marriage as strangers to each other. The older system provided them with a clearly defined role to play in marriage. Today, the old certainties are gone, and marriage involves negotiated roles and constitutes a greater challenge to the partners' individual strengths and the bond between the couple. In our next chapter we shall examine how our couples survived the transition from courtship to marriage.

CHAPTER FOUR

Negotiating Roles in Marriage

In this chapter we shall examine how our subjects actually fared in marriage. In our opening chapter, we reviewed the shift in the understanding of marriage as an institution, based on clearly defined roles for each spouse, to an understanding of marriage as a more fluid reality. This less rigid concept of marriage emphasises personal fulfilment achieved through a close interpersonal, affective union. The impact of this change has been profound. What was previously regarded as a satisfactory marriage may not meet current criteria. Traditional priorities, such as children, financial security and the absence of cruelty, are still valued in marriage. However, today much more is sought in marital relationships. The current concept of marriage includes the expectation that both partners will share in all aspects of the relationship: decision-making, financial control, caring for children, and, the building of an affective union. The option of leaving an unsatisfactory marriage is available and frequently chosen.

Social change is rarely lateral or uniform across all members of society. Marriage is a major institution is Irish society and while marriage may have changed, it is unlikely that everyone has accepted this change or sought to apply it to their own marriage or lifestyle. In this chapter, we shall examine the degree to which our subjects accepted a negotiated concept of marriage in practice. We shall focus particularly on any differences that may emerge between men and women in this regard. Personal fulfilment is a nebulous concept and clear criteria for its achievement are impossible to find. However, it is generally accepted that a close bond between the couple is a prerequisite for its attainment in marriage.

The records of the Galway Regional Marriage Tribunal contain information on our couples' experience of marriage. Specific questions are devoted to the major issues and problem areas in marriage. In addition, interviewees frequently draw attention to factors which they regard as important, but which may not be adverted to in the standard questionnaire. Consequently, our data includes a lot of information regarding the major issues in our subjects' marriages as described by the participants, and their lay and professional witnesses. In chapter two, we considered our subjects from a demographic perspective and presented data on the ages of our subjects on entry into marriage, the number of children resulting from each union and the duration of the marriages. In this chapter, we shall comment on the qualitative aspects of the marriages. In particular, we will focus on the factors associated with the destabilisation of the marital relationship.

This chapter will consist of six sections and a general conclusion. These sections are based on the problems identified by our couples and their witnesses. Figure 4.1[1] presents these factors according to the number of cases in which each factor is mentioned and we shall order this discussion accordingly.

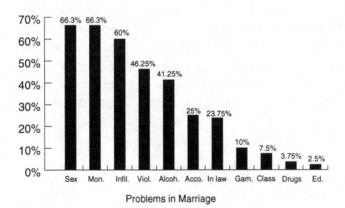

Figure 4.1 Problems in Marriage

SEXUAL PROBLEMS

In the course of their interview with the Marriage Tribunal, the spouses comment on their sexual relationship in marriage. The frankness of both men and women in commenting on the most intimate aspect of their marriage is notable. The contrast with the reserve among O'Higgins' 1974 subjects indicates a new openness regarding sex, and is in itself a sociological fact.[2] In a majority of cases (66%) at least one partner described this aspect of the marriage as unsatisfactory. While the distinction between cause and symptom is not always clear, it is evident that in most cases the sexual problems reflected, rather than caused, the marital problems.

In many cases, the sexual relationship only became an issue towards the end of the marriage, when breakdown was already well advanced. The following comment typifies such cases: 'At the end, I started getting very turned off and always had a diplomatic headache.' Others clearly link the sexual problem with another issue, such as alcohol abuse. In these cases, the sexual problem is a manifestation of another problem rather than an issue in itself.

A closer study of our sample reveals that in nineteen cases (23.7%) there were problems in the sexual sphere *per se*. In these cases the problems were present from early in the marriage and are perceived by at least one partner as having played a major role in the breakdown of the relationship. A further subdivision is possible. In twelve marriages, the problem took the form of one party having little or no interest in pursuing a sexual relationship with her/his spouse. For six couples, the problem consisted in one party not respecting the wishes of the other regarding the frequency or nature of their sexual relationship. One case can not be clearly assigned to either sub-group. Table 4.1 presents this information.

Problems in sexual area	Percentage	Number of cases
Sexual relationship depicted as unsatisfactory	66%	53
Problems in sexual relationship *per se*	23.7%	19
Diminished interest in sexual relationship	15%	12
Unacceptable sexual practices	7.5%	6
Residual	1.25%	1

Table 4.1 Sexual Problems in Marriage

Diminished interest in the sexual relationship

We shall begin with a consideration of the twelve couples whose sexual relationship was troubled due to a lack of desire by a spouse. In nine cases the indifferent or hostile partner was the woman.[3] The most common explanation offered by women for their lack of interest was the absence of emotional attraction. A woman who was pressurised by her family to marry is typical of many. She stated:

> I did not love [him] … I was acting … on the wedding night, I avoided sexual relations … I said to myself that if I did not have sexual relations, I would have a way out of the marriage.

The couple had not been sexually involved before marriage. The husband corroborated his wife' evidence: 'She was very emotional, cried half the wedding night. She wanted no sexual relationship … she never acknowledged me as her husband.'

Though the marriage was eventually consummated, the sexual relationship was never satisfactory. In the husband's words: 'She never wanted me to touch her and would cry after we made love. She couldn't bear me to give her an affectionate hug.'

In two cases, the woman retained an attachment to a previous boyfriend. In one such case the man stated: 'She [had] no interest in sex … it was six months before we consummated our marriage … we only had sex five or six times.' The evidence depicts the wife as having married an older man in pursuit of material wealth. She conducted a relationship with a man of her own age before, during and after the marriage.

A fulfilling sexual relationship in courtship was not always predictive of a similar experience in marriage. This is evident in the case of a couple whose marriage was precipitated by the birth of their child. Both agree that there were no problems in their premarital sexual relationship. Yet, after marriage the woman lost interest in sex. Both parties see her attachment to her previous boyfriend as the principal cause of her change in attitude and the marriage ended when she went to live with him. Two pregnant brides stated that they lost interest in sex after childbirth. In both cases, the husband's response served to further undermine the relationship. One of the women stated: 'I lost all interest in sex. [His] response was that he would look for it elsewhere.' The lack of an emotive bond emerges as the key issue in these cases.

As discussed previously, victims of child sexual abuse frequently encounter problems in adult sexual relationships. Six participants in our study (five female and one male) stated that they experienced sexual abuse as children; all six referred to problems in the sexual arena in their adult lives.

Diminished interest in sex was not exclusively a female phenomenon. In three marriages, the male partner suffered a loss of interest in intercourse. One man stated the reasons for the decline in the couple's sexual relationship in succinct terms: 'I was losing interest in her.'

In one case, psychological problems were offered as the explanation for the man's lack of interest in the sexual relationship.

A fear of pregnancy is cited as the cause of the deterioration of another couple's sexual relationship. The woman stated: 'I was conscious of not wanting to get pregnant again ... we were not very sexually active.' Her husband concurred: 'We were both terrified that she'd get pregnant again and we couldn't afford another child ... [our sexual relationship] deteriorated.' This couple's attitude towards contraception was not explored. Within a short time, the husband became involved in another sexual relationship.

The principal reason for diminished interest in sexual relations is the absence of affective feelings. In most cases, the decision to marry was rushed and not entirely free. The absence of a close affective bond rendered sexual relations unattractive and in some cases repulsive for women. In the cases of the men who had diminished interest in sexual relations, the reasons vary. Two men entered marriage hastily or as the result of pressure and appear to have had no emotional feeling for their wives and both men became sexually involved with other women. Another suffered from a psychological disorder. The sexual problem was a major destabilising factor in the marriages considered in this section. The origins of the problem in the vast majority of cases was emotional rather than physical. Marriage and sexual intimacy within marriage is increasingly linked to emotive feelings of love: in its absence many women and some men have grave difficulty in accepting sexual intimacy.

Unacceptable sexual practices

Sexual difficulties occasionally took the form of one partner ignoring the wishes of the other. In some cases, this appears to have been inspired more by selfishness than aggression. The comments of one husband reflects a number of marriages: 'I never satisfied her sexually ... the predominant part of the sexual relationship was me satisfying myself, as quickly as possible.' Both parties agree that their sexual relationship ended after a few years, after which the man became unfaithful. These cases are characterised by a lack of concern for the feelings of the other partner, rather than anything more sinister.

In six cases the sexual problems were more serious. Some men insisted on having sexual intercourse despite the objections of their wives, a situation which was tantamount to rape. Other partners insisted on practices which the other found objectionable. These marriages were characterised by varying degrees and forms of violence.

Pornography and psychological violence were features of some marriages. One wife described her husband as 'unbelievably demanding in terms of sexual intimacy. He saw it as love ... he saw it as the number one thing in life. How I felt didn't matter. He had hard core pornographic books and films.'

In some cases the violence was verbal and emotional. One woman states: 'He kept telling me that I was frigid. [He] combined all this with being jealous of me. If he saw me talking to a man, then I was a prostitute.'

Some men displayed a lack of appreciation of medical problems experienced by their wives. One woman stated: 'Sexual intercourse became very painful for me. It related to my health problems but [my husband] would never accept that and he often forced his way.' Her husband denied these allegations and referred to personality problems on the part of the woman. The violence involved in marital rape was frequently extreme and the sexual practices dangerous and degrading. One woman stated: 'He actually tried to insert an [object] in my vagina. It was horrible.' The husband denies these allegations. A common feature in the cases in this paragraph is that sexual intercourse ceased to be a reflection of a loving relationship and became a form of control or self indulgence for the man.

The explanations offered for unacceptable sexual practices in marriage vary considerably. In two cases, there is evidence that one or other party suffered from a psychological or personality disorder.

Sexual and other forms of violence was frequently present in marriages characterised by psychological problems. Marital rape was often linked with alcohol abuse. One woman described how her husband 'came in very drunk ... busted my bedroom door and forced sex on me. You could call it rape.'

These cases are characterised by the absence of a functioning marital relationship. The issues involved are more closely related to spousal abuse than sexuality as commonly understood.

In summary, these cases are characterised by the sexual demands of the man being unacceptable to the woman. These demands were accompanied by varying degrees of violence. A link with other issues, primarily alcohol abuse and psychological disorders, also emerged from our discussion. The sexual relationship ceased to be an expression of the couple's emotional commitment, and became an assertion of power and served to undermine the marriage.

Response to sexual problems in marriage

A male-female divergence in responding to sexual problems is evident in our sample. Most men responded to the lack of a sexual relationship by effectively withdrawing from the marriage. This took various forms. One woman stated: '[He] made unhappy by [the lack of sex and] began to spend more time away from me, often returning to his family ... He began to drink heavily and secretly.'

Withdrawal frequently involved infidelity. One husband made this link explicit: 'Our sexual relationship declined ... I found other ladies attractive.' The physical rather than the emotive aspect of sexual involvement emerged as being of primary importance to many men. The effective withdrawal of these men from the marriage placed its future in doubt.

The response of women centred on feelings and emotions. In the small number of cases where the man lost interest in sex, the wife experienced feelings of rejection. The following comment is typical: 'He had no interest. I felt rejected.'

In the more extreme cases involving marital rape, terms such as 'disgusting' and 'repugnant' are employed by women to describe to their husbands and the sexual aspect of the marriage. One woman stated that, after her husband raped her, 'my feeling for him were indescribable. I hated him.'

Many victims of sexual violence were reluctant to seek outside help. A woman whose husband subjected her to sexual practices that placed her health in danger stated: 'I was afraid to tell the doctor ... I was too embarrassed.'

The absence of attempts to address jointly the problems in the sexual area of the marriage is notable. There are few references to couples seeking professional help focused on this aspect of their marriage. The extreme nature of the violence present in some cases, and the lack of emotional involvement by a partner to many of the marriages, is relevant here. The desire, and frequently the ability, to address the problem was absent.

Conclusion

We identified two principal categories of sexual problems. One involved a lack of interest by one partner, usually the woman. This was usually due to the absence of an affective bond between the couple. The other category involved one partner, in our study always the man, making sexual demands which the other partner was unwilling or unable to accommodate. Verbal, psychological and physical violence frequently accompanied these demands.

On the descriptive level, both men and women viewed the sexual relationship as much more than simply a means of reproduction. The trend of attaching ever increasing significance to the pleasurable aspect of sexual intercourse, which O'Higgins noted in 1974, is firmly established in our study.[4] Sexual problems emerged as a barometer of other problems in the marriage, rather than a major cause of the unhappiness in themselves. Problems in the overall relationship were reflected in the sexual relationship, which in turn served to exasperate the problems which had caused the sexual difficulties.

Individual factors, frequently alcohol addiction or personality disorders, often accentuated sexual problems. The current understanding of marriage envisages sexual relations as reflecting and re-enforcing the emotive bond between the couple. In our study, this understanding appears to be more prevalent among women than men. A male-female duality is detectable, in that men are more likely to emphasise quantity, while women are prone to stress quality. The theme of strangers on an affective level, committing themselves to a form of marriage dependant on an affective union, is dominant in this section.

MATERIAL ASPECTS OF MARRIAGE

Financial problems were mentioned in 66% of cases. Accommodation occurs less frequently (25%). Work was rarely mentioned in isolation and will be considered in conjunction with financial issues. As in the case of sexual problems, financial and accommodation issues were closely related to other problems. The issue of cause and symptom emerges once again. However, though mentioned by a very large number of participants as problematic, very few couples regarded these issues as being of decisive importance in the breakdown of their marriages.

Finance: Income related problems

Financial problems had two dominant aspects: inadequate income and inappropriate spending. For some couples, the problem was a combination of both aspects. In some cases, the financial problems merely reflected the strain of making a living. The following comment typifies many: '[At times] we earned a lot of money. There were lean periods, and [she] was often annoyed with me over this.'

In these marriages, the financial issue was not a significant problem. In more serious cases, the financial problems took the form of one partner not making adequate provision for ordinary domestic expenditure. One woman stated: '[He] never gave me any money towards the running of the house.'

In many cases, financial problems were linked to deception and laziness. One woman stated:

[He was] very lazy. He took to the bed ... he loved to watch TV ... The huge issue between us was money. I was paying the day-to-day expenses. [He] was responsible for [utilities] ... I was putting money into a [bank] account, he would have drawn it out before I could sign a cheque for a bill ... I didn't know the extent [of his deceit] until we separated.

In these cases the emphasis is on the lack of honesty in the relationship, rather than the financial issue *per se*. Unemployment, or a reluctance to work, occurs in many cases. A husband stated: 'We were [both] drawing social welfare. I went out, most days, looking for a job ... [She] refused to work and this annoyed me a lot.' However, in explaining the failure of their relationship, both parties point to interpersonal factors rather than the financial issue.

Some couples suffered financial problems due to failure in business. In one case the woman stated: 'There was a business failure ... He mortgaged our house to raise money... I had no option. He was a domineering person.'

The evidence depicts the financial uncertainty as symptomatic, rather than causative, of the problems that led to instability in the marriage.

Finance: Expenditure related problems

Problems on the expenditure side were usually related to other issues, most frequently alcohol abuse. One woman placed the financial problems in context. She stated: 'We never had money. It was a problem but not the biggest problem. I was working, so I had a few pounds.' Her husband is frank in his evidence: 'I drank money that was needed urgently in the home ... This gave rise to a lot of arguments between us.'

Irresponsible spending was not limited to men. A witness stated: '[Her] spending was excessive ... you would see a cab calling for her maybe three times a day ... she spent money buying [luxuries].'

In another case, financial gain was seen as the motivation for the marriage. This marriage involved excessive spending and fraud by the woman. However, a lack of affection, rather than the financial problems, are depicted as causing breakdown.

In most cases, there is a clear link between financial problems and other difficulties, usually alcohol abuse, unwillingness to work, or lack of communication and trust. Financial problems are frequently the focus of tension in the marriage, but are never presented as the principal problem. The fact that, in the majority of marriages, both parties had an independent source of income helped alleviate the financial problems.

Accommodation

While accommodation is mentioned as a problem in 25% of cases, it was not regarded as being of crucial importance in any marriage. A small number of couples lived with in-laws. The reaction of one man is this situation is typical: 'I wasn't comfortable in her home.'

Some accommodation was inadequate or over-crowded. One woman stated: 'The flat was a shambles ... damp and cold. After being there for just a couple of weeks, our baby developed a chest infection.' A couple lost their family home due to failure in business. Another failed to agree on whether to live in Ireland or abroad and never established a joint domicile.

Accommodation in itself did not play a decisive role in the marriages under review. Where it did emerge as a problem it was a minor source of dissatisfaction. It served as an indicator of deeper problems rather than as a problem in itself. No participant in the study saw accommodation issues as decisive in the failure of the marriage.

Conclusion

Money, work and accommodation were *foci* of discord in a majority of marriages. However, despite the frequency with which these problems were mentioned they rarely emerged as independent causes of breakdown. Other problems found tangible expression through these factors. Problems such as personal irresponsibility, the pursuance of a single lifestyle in marriage, excessive drinking and difficulties in decision-making and communication often led to financial problems. Material issues frequently reflected personal problems and inherent weaknesses in the interpersonal relationship, and in turn frequently served to accentuate the problems that helped cause them. A failure to adjust to marriage is apparent in this section – the couples failed to negotiate mutually satisfactory roles. It appears likely that a well functioning marital relationship would successfully address problems in these areas.

INFIDELITY

All the members of our sample celebrated their marriages according to the Catholic rite which emphasises fidelity. However, infidelity was a feature of many of the cases. In this study, we shall regard infidelity as referring to an inappropriate relationship between a married person and another adult, while the married person continues to reside with his/her spouse. This description includes all relationships which were regarded by the other spouse as a threat to the marriage. However, it excludes relationships which began after the married couple separated.

Infidelity is mentioned in forty-eight marriages (60%) in our study. This figure is unusually high. The 1994 annual report from Accord, Dublin[5] lists infidelity as a presenting problem in 17.6% of cases. A.I.M. reports a figure of 25%[6], Eamon Murphy 32%[7], and M.R.C.S., 18%.[8] The discrepancy requires explanation. Our broad definition of infidelity, which includes relationships that may not have been sexual, serves to inflate our percentage. Our figure also includes all cases where infidelity is mentioned and consequently some references are allegations which may have no basis in fact. Infidelity in the form of meeting an alternative partner is often the final stimulus towards separation in a marriage which had already broken down. The Marriage Tribunal deals only with couples who have abandoned hope of reconciliation and therefore will include more such relationships. The counselling agencies help couples who are working to salvage their marriages and who are therefore less likely to have met an alternative partner.[9] The distinction between a presenting problem and a detailed analysis of the mar-

riage is also pertinent. A common reaction to adultery is denial.[10]
The agencies listed above rely on information volunteered by the
partners and are frequently limited to speaking to one partner.[11]
The Marriage Tribunal receives information from witnesses and
therefore is more likely to overcome denial. These factors explain, at
least in substantive fashion, the apparent discrepancy identified
above.

Infidelity in marriage

Among our subjects, men are slightly more likely than women to be
unfaithful. Twenty-five men (31%) are described as unfaithful. The
equivalent figure for women is twenty-two (27.5%). In four marriages, both partners are described as unfaithful. A considerable
variation is detectable in terms of the nature of the inappropriate
relationship. Table 4.2 presents this data.

Infidelity in Marriage	Percentage	Number of cases
At least one party unfaithful	60%	48
Man unfaithful	31%	25
Woman unfaithful	27%	22
Both Parties unfaithful	5%	4

Table 4.2 Infidelity in Marriage

In some marriages, the allegation of infidelity arises from one partner's reaction to what the other regarded as normal socialising. The
wife in one such case stated: 'I was working late ... one of the guys
from the office and I decided to get a bite to eat ... When I got in, he
started calling me names. He jumped on top of me ... I called the
police.'

In other cases the relationship can be characterised as infatuation. One woman stated: 'I became attracted to a man ... [he] was
not aware of my feelings for him.

Several witnesses commented on the detrimental impact that
inappropriate, albeit non-sexual, relationships had on the marriages concerned. The following comment is typical:

[She] wore very short dresses and used to drink ... the way she behaved led to men inviting her out … she had fun in a sleazy sort of way. I'm not suggesting that there was anything sexual involved … [Her husband] reacted by becoming nasty and extremely jealous.

In these cases there is evidence of pre-existing strain in the marriage. The behaviour of one partner and the reaction of the other reflected an inability to discuss problems and a deficiency in emotional intimacy.

In some marriages infidelity consisted of one incident of extra-marital sexual intimacy. The wife in one such marriage stated: 'The only example of [his] infidelity that I am aware of is one night that he spent with a waitress … infidelity wasn't a major problem.'

In several cases where women engaged in 'one night stands', special circumstances were present. A wife stated:

[My husband] was unbelievably demanding in terms of [sex]: He kept telling me that I was frigid … I went with a fellow for one night … I was trying to convince myself that I was not frigid.

In these cases the marriage was under strain due to other factors. The infidelity usually occurred in the context of a marital relationship which had already broken down.

Infidelity also took the form of serial, superficial relationships. One wife provided the following description: 'If I was playing with a [sports] team … he would end up having affairs with some of the players.'

Promiscuity also had health implications: 'Three times I got VD from him … it was from promiscuity.' Though less prevalent, some women are also depicted as promiscuous. In one case a witness stated: 'She was seeing various fellows … she was using them to have a good time.'

Infidelity in this form was frequently only one of several problems afflicting the marriage. Most partners who engaged in a plurality of superficial relationships were male and all show evidence of a failure to assume the responsibilities of marriage.

Some of our subjects became involved in a long term relationship. Women were most likely to form this type of relationship and several resumed a relationship with a previous boyfriend.

Frequently, the new relationship endured after the end of the marriage. A husband stated: '[She] got to know this guy and she told me that she was leaving me for him ... She and [he] are still together.'

In these situations a push-pull dynamic is at work. The attractions of the alternative relationship are at least as important in precipitating breakdown as the problems in the marriage.

In summary, we can state that the form of infidelity varied considerably. The scope extended from non-sexual, emotional dependency to superficial sexual liaisons, to long-term associations involving commitment and mutual emotional investment. The latter two were most common. Superficial relationships were more typical of men, while women were most likely to engage in long-term relationships that frequently endured after marriage. For women, a new relationship frequently served to highlight dissatisfaction with the marital relationship and encouraged her to leave the marriage.

The reaction of the other spouse

Infidelity constitutes a major crisis in marriage. Inappropriate relationships were usually conducted, initially at least, in secret. The reaction of the other spouse only occurred on his/her discovery of the affair. Some were reluctant to believe that their spouse was unfaithful. One woman stated: '[He] was unfaithful ... People told me ... [He] had often said to me that he would kill me, if I was unfaithful to him ... I was slow to believe [it]. He denied it.'

Some adopted a fatalistic approach. A man described his wife's reaction as follows: '[My wife] knew that I was playing around but she wouldn't complain to me ... She probably decided that it wouldn't make any difference.'

Infidelity occasionally impacted on the health of the other party. A wife described the tension involved: 'I suffered headaches and I was not eating or sleeping properly.'

Some marriages survived for some time after the revelation/discovery of the infidelity. A husband stated: 'I had a one night stand ... [My wife] found out. We talked it out and our relationship recovered.' However, the husband continued to be unfaithful and the marriage collapsed. This pattern is reflected in several marriages.

Many women reacted in a direct fashion: 'I was devastated … I packed his bags and told him to go.'

In all cases, infidelity placed the future of the marriage in doubt. From our discussion it is evident that considerable reserves of personal strength on the part of both parties and unity between the couple are required to survive such a major crisis. Our couples were ill-equipped to cope with the task.

Context of infidelity

In our study infidelity always occurred in the context of several other problems in the marriage. A selectivity factor may apply here. Infidelity *per se* is not a ground for nullity. Therefore, applications to the tribunal where infidelity was the only problem are unlikely to proceed past the *prima facie* stage.[12]

In cases involving infidelity other pre-existing problems are usually cited. In one marriage a witness referred to the couple's incompatibility: 'She needed to marry someone who had a more open mind. [She] hadn't the freedom to be herself … [he] suffocated her.' Most men place their infidelity in the context of a dysfunctional marriage. The following comment is typical: 'I lost interest in her … I lived in pubs and I went with various women.' A lack of unity between the couple and insufficient commitment to the marriage is evident in these cases.

Various other contexts are also cited. An association is occasionally posited between the decline of the marital sexual relationship and infidelity. One wife stated: 'I did my level best to please him [sexually] … he was seeing one particular girl … he is now living with [her].'

Another man depicted his extramarital relationship as healthy: 'I used her as a safety valve … I didn't really care about her … it was sexual … it was therapeutic, like squash or golf. Others link infidelity to new-found affluence: 'I did the things I always wanted to do because I had money.' Several young husbands refer to the problems in 'settling down' at so early an age: 'I was young … there were lots of girls available.'

In our discussion of alcohol abuse, we referred to the link

between it and infidelity. Some men referred to an inherent problem with the notion of fidelity: 'I never contemplated being faithful
... I could see no harm in having an affair ... so long as I am pre-
pared to live with the consequences.'

Sometimes infidelity is linked to family of origin. An unfaithful
husband stated: 'Fidelity was never a big thing for me. I hadn't seen
it growing up.'

An inability to lead a monogamous life is alleged in the case of
only one woman.

In these cases, the unfaithful partner is characterised as grossly
immature and an unwillingness or an inability to deal with the
challenges of marriage is evident.

In most cases where both partners were unfaithful, infidelity by
one partner is presented as reaction to that of the other. In these
cases the separation was all but inevitable by the time the second
partner became unfaithful.

The reasons advanced for infidelity varied from pre-existing
problems in the relationship to an inherent inability to be faithful.
Unfaithful partners rarely accepted personal responsibility for their
actions and tended to quote mitigating circumstances. The other
partner was more inclined to apportion culpability. While it is not
possible to disentangle cause and effect between infidelity and
other problems in marriage, it is clear that infidelity almost always
arose in the context of an unhappy marriage. Our subjects lacked
the personal resources and their relationships were too feeble to
survive the challenge. Infidelity served to accentuate the unhappiness
and frequently brought it to crisis point.

Conclusion

Infidelity constitutes a major crisis in marriage. Some marriages
involving infidelity survived for a short time. However, in our sample, ongoing infidelity made separation inevitable. The present
study, by its nature, does not all allow for definitive conclusions
regarding the impact of infidelity on marital stability. By definition,
all the marriages in our study ended in separation, and therefore it
is not possible to access accurately the nature of the challenge posed
by infidelity to the stability of marriage.

We have uncovered considerable evidence that infidelity is frequently a symptom of pre-existing problems in the communication and emotional areas of marriage. The marriages cited above were subject to several problems. Most unfaithful spouses appeared to lack commitment to the marriage or belief in fidelity. Male infidelity usually took the form of engaging in several relationships of short duration, while women tended to become involved in a long term relationship which frequently endured after separation. This characterisation is not absolute; we found examples of promiscuous wives and of husbands who became involved in a committed, long term, extramarital relationship.

While infidelity is rarely the starting point for marital problems, it is frequently the catalyst for separation. It is likely that a shared causality is present. An immature or uncommitted partner to a precarious marriage, is likely to engage in several forms of behaviour which undermine the marriage further. Alcohol abuse, lack of communication, lack of companionship and inappropriate relationships, frequently occur together in various permutations. A failure to negotiate mutually satisfactory roles, and the persistence of some older cultural norms, is evident in this section. For our subjects, infidelity is still regarded as incompatible with marriage; this is evident in the subterfuge engaged in by the 'offender' and the reaction of the other party. The more flexible role of spouse does not extend to having multiple sexual partners.

VIOLENCE

Violence is mentioned as a feature in the breakdown of thirty-seven marriages in our study (46%). With one exception, all complainants are female. Within these thirty-seven marriages there is a wide variation. Some involved sustained, frequent and severe violence, while others involved a single, relatively minor incident of violence, such as pushing, at a time when the relationship had already brokendown. The following is an example of a marriage where the violence was infrequent and relatively minor. The woman stated:

When I went home, he said 'where are you until now?' I told

> him. He said 'I don't believe you' and he took the brush to hit
> me. I ran to the car ... I got a place of my own.

In these marriages, the violence is the final straw which precipitated
breakdown. The relationship *per se* had already broken down; the
incident of violence convinced the victim that all hope of rebuilding
the marriage had vanished.

Descriptions and rationalisations of violence in marriage

As descriptions of violence in marriage are frequently accompanied
by rationalisations, it is appropriate to treat both together. Fifteen
marriages (19%) involved prolonged and extreme violence. Many
victims were unable to explain the presence of violence in their
marriages. These women concentrated on describing the violence
and do not attempt to explain why it occurred. One such woman
stated: 'I will never know why the violence started ... Alcohol
wasn't a problem, we hadn't enough money for that ... As regards
verbal abuse, he was very hurtful.' Her brother provided a more
detailed description:

> Before they got married there used to be fairly lively rows ...
> after they married it got a lot worse. He used to get really, really
> angry. He would shout and scream and become violent towards
> [his wife] ... He threw her down the stairs. He would beat her
> over not having the dinner ready.

In some cases, violence occurred even during pregnancy.

These women merely described the violence. The only explanation they offered is their husbands' wish to exercise total control
over them.

Some women had more developed thoughts as to the aetiology
of the violence. Several linked excessive drinking to violent behaviour. The following are a sample of comments by these women: 'He
was really drunk ... He was crazy, just shouting and roaring. He
beat on the door and dragged me out, his eyes were mental.'

A medical doctor supported the link between alcohol abuse and
spousal violence: 'A major problem was [the husband's] alcohol
intake and the physical abuse which he meted out to [his wife]
under such influence.'

Violence also impinged on the sexual dimension of marriage. The next comment typifies the experience of many victims: 'He came in drunk ... and forced sex on me.'

Psychological or personality disorders were also linked to spousal abuse. In some relationships, where psychological disorders were present, the violence pre-dated marriage. In a case which included professional evidence of the man's psychological problems, the wife stated:

There was violence pre-marriage ... one day you could discuss something with him and get on fine, the next day if you raised the same subject, he might react in a violent way. The violence got worse as time went by. Sometimes, he hit me to see me cry.

In these cases, the violence was extreme.

In summary, we can state that while some women were unable to explain their husband's violence, most pointed to a specific cause, the most common being alcohol abuse. Psychological problems were also advanced as an explanation, albeit less frequently. In many cases, violence was triggered by a trivial matter. The description of the violence was frequently harrowing and included sexual violence and other forms of physical injury.

Comments of violent spouses

The reaction of the men when confronted with their wife's allegations of physical violence varied. Many totally denied it. The following comment is representative of many: 'I didn't get violent ... we had plenty of verbal rows but nothing else.' A victim described how her husband coped with his violence: 'The following day, he would claim that he couldn't remember being violent.'

Denial was the most common reaction to allegations of violence. Others admitted a limited amount of violence. In a case where the wife's claims of severe and sustained spousal abuse are corroborated by witnesses, the man insisted that: 'There was one violent incident which took place just before we separated. That was all.'

Another man felt that his wife over-reacted to the violence in the marriage:

There were four or five incidents. There was violence from both

sides, pretty much always started by her. It wouldn't be real
bad, just stupid pushing and shoving. But she would [say] I was
trying to kill her.

The witnesses depicted the man as the instigator of the violence and
represented it in more severe terms than admitted by him. While
the bitterness instilled by separation can lead to exaggeration on the
part of the aggrieved spouse, it is clear that several of these men
grossly understated the nature and impact of their violent behaviour. In a rare case where violence was admitted, the man appeared
fatalistic regarding the prospects of change.

The comments of those accused of violence tend to be brief.
They do not include details regarding the nature of the violence or
evidence of reflection on the causes or impact of the violence. The
most common reaction of those accused of violence is partial or
total denial.

Effects on victims

The tribunal files contain descriptions of the impact of spousal violence on the victims. In all cases the impact is severe. A medical doctor
described the effect that violence had on one victim's mental health:
'There was physical, mental and verbal abuse, to the extend that it
was wearing [her] nerves, with associated weight loss, insomnia
and anxiety.' In another case, the victim provided a similar description: 'My mental health began to suffer; I found it hard to sleep and
sometimes had nightmares.'

Physical violence was usually accompanied by verbal violence.
Some women regarded the verbal aggression as more degrading
than the physical violence. One woman stated: 'The violence and
verbal abuse ... was there all throughout the marriage ... The verbal
abuse was much worse that the other.'

Many women saw violence as the final straw in the breakdown
of the marriage. Many women stated that violence led to a complete
change in their feelings towards their husbands, frequently to the
point of hatred. One woman concluded her description of a particularly violent incident by stating: 'That was our final separation.'

In summary, the impact of violence on the victims was twofold.

Many women suffered in terms of their mental health and self-confidence. The second effect was a reversal in the victim's feelings for her husband, which convinced her that separation was the only option.

Response of victims

Many women attempted to reason with the violent husband and encourage him to avail of counselling. The wife of an alcoholic and violent husband stated: 'He promised me he would join AA ... He never did.' Many sought the protection of the police or courts. Another woman, on the advice of a friend, took legal action: 'I got a severe beating ... I didn't want anyone to know. A [friend] said "You are coming to a solicitor with me." I applied for a barring order, because I was petrified.'

Some women admitted to retaliating with violence. One woman states in response to her husband's violence: 'I hit him back an odd time.' Another woman stated that her reaction to her husband's physical and verbal abuse was confined to verbal insults: 'I probably said something to him, but not as nasty as he was.' Other women reacted in a more extreme fashion including feelings of hatred and bitterness. One such women stated: 'I often planned ways of actually killing him.'

Most women were embarrassed at the existence of violence in their marriages. Some had married against the advice of family or friends and found it difficult to admit that they had made a misguided decision. A catalyst was frequently required to enable the women to act. The urgings of a friend or the involvement of a member of a caring profession was often such a catalyst. Some victims reached the point where the violence was intolerable and they were compelled to act. Others were propelled into action by their children being exposed to the risk of, or actually experiencing, violence. Some women, through their own economic resources or the help of family or friends, were able to leave the family home and consider the next appropriate step to take. Others did not have this option and relied on the protective aspects of family law and sought protection or barring orders.

Conclusion

Spousal abuse is the antithesis of marriage, understood as a union based on love. In some cases violence pre-dated the marriage. These marriages usually took place in the context of some form of pressure. In most cases, the spousal abuse commenced on marriage and served to placed the future of the union in doubt.[13] Frequently, a link with alcohol abuse or psychological disorder was evident. In our data, the reaction of the accused varied from denial to a limited admission. The effect on the victim often included injury to her physical and mental health and feelings of hatred towards her husband. However, many women continued to endure violence for long periods usually due to low self-esteem, an unwillingness to admit the violent nature of the marriage, a lack of financial independence, the hope that the violence was only a temporary phenomenon, a belief in the permanence of marriage, or a desire not to become a one parent family. Ultimately the victims reacted and, frequently with the help of friends, the Gardaí, caring agencies or the courts, terminated cohabitation. Violent marriages reinforce the picture of couples entering marriage without establishing a close interpersonal bond.

ALCOHOL AND OTHER ADDICTIONS

In this section, we shall explore the effect of three addictions on marriage: alcohol, gambling and drugs. Alcoholism is the most common addiction and is mentioned in thirty-three cases, which constitutes 41% of the sample. While not all these marriages were characterised by alcoholism, in all cases alcohol is perceived as a problem. The other two addictions affected few marriages; gambling occurred in eight cases (10% of the sample) and drugs in four cases (5%). We shall examine how the abuse of alcohol, drugs or gambling impacted on the marriages concerned. We shall review the statements of both parties and the opinions expressed by the witnesses concerning these problems.

Alcohol abuse

Excessive drinking emerged from our study as primarily a male problem. Twenty-eight men (35%) and ten women (12.5%) are depicted as drinking to excess. There is a ratio of almost 3:1 between male and female excessive drinkers. In five marriages both parties are regarded as having a drink problem. Within the thirty-three marriages affected, there is a considerable variation between situations where one or other party was clearly an alcoholic and situations where the person, though a heavy drinker, does not appear to be addicted. Our primary concern is the impact of excessive drinking on the ability of the couple to establish and maintain a sustainable marriage. Table 4.3 present this data.

Addictions in Marriage	Percentage	Number of cases
Alcohol abuse: marriages affected	41.25%	33
Husbands abusing alcohol	35%	28
Wives abusing alcohol	12.5%	10
Both parties abusing alcohol	6.25%	5
Gambling: marriages affected	10%	8

Table 4.3 Addictions in Marriage

Alcohol abuse in men

An association between excessive drinking among men and spousal abuse is apparent in our sample. Of the twenty-eight marriages involving excessive drinking by the husband, seventeen (60.7%) are also described as violent. This contrasts with 40% for the entire sample. Excessive drinking was also associated with more extreme violence. While not all male heavy drinkers are depicted as violent, an association is evident.

An excessive drinker accepted that there was an association between his drinking and his aggressive behaviour towards his wife. He stated: 'All the things that were wrong in me would come out in drink … [My wife] was scared of me. I made life hell … I'd be full of tension.' This point was detailed in our section on violence in marriage.

Alcohol abuse also impacted on companionship in marriage. All but two of the twenty-eight intemperate male drinkers in the sample drank outside the home. The two exceptions lived abroad and one was foreign. Excessive drinkers tended to socialise without their wives and thereby severely reduced or eliminated shared social life. Alcohol abuse also impaired a person's ability to communicate on a meaningful level. By impacting negatively on companionship and communication between husband and wife, excessive drinking served to undermine the marriage.

Reduced companionship was compounded by a deterioration in trust between the partners. A woman illustrated the point as follows: 'He is an exceptional liar, very convincing and a lot of people believed him. I did for a long time. I think it goes with being an alcoholic.'

Marriage understood as a free partnership requires trust to survive. Therefore, the negative impact of excessive drinking on trust in marriage is noteworthy.

In addition, alcohol abuse frequently led to irrational or socially unacceptable behaviour. One woman described how, due to her husband's behaviour,

> there was blood and broken glass all over the floor. I threatened to leave him. He threatened to kill himself and [he] cut his wrist. He went to a treatment centre. While there he was unfaithful to me ... I left him.

The behaviour associated with alcohol abuse served to place the marriages concerned under intolerable strain.

Excessive drinking also led to health problems on the part of the person concerned and financial problems for the family. In a marriage where the man's drinking was facilitated by his employment both factors were present. His wife stated:

> He drank in relation to work and would come home drunk and he also drank at home ... [He had] all the classic symptoms of alcoholism ... he went completely berserk with drink ... He would be violently sick for a couple of days ... his short term memory was affected ...

In a marriage where both partners drank heavily, the husband alluded to the financial impact: 'It wasn't so much what we were drinking as that we couldn't afford it.'

The effects depicted above, in the areas of health and employment, occurred in the more extreme cases.

In several cases, a link is suggested between excessive drinking and infidelity. Fifteen men who drank heavily are depicted as unfaithful. This represents 53.5% of the sub-sample and contrasts with 35% of the men in the total sample who are described as unfaithful. One man stated, under the influence of alcohol, 'my true nature would break out. I had lots of girlfriends.' Several cases contain an association between excessive drinking and casual sexual encounters.

Male alcohol abuse frequently undermined the marital relationship. The impact occurred in the areas of finance, companionship, trust, violence, and fidelity. In all cases where the husband drank to excess, his drinking is depicted as a decisive factor in the deterioration of the marriage.

Alcohol abuse in women

Intemperate drinking was less common among females. Ten women are described as drinking to excess. The impact on marriage resembles that described above. Financial implications, the deterioration of companionship and the increased likelihood of infidelity are common to both groups. Violence was not a feature of the women in our study, except as retaliation to male violence.

Lack of companionship and irrational behaviour became evident in the life of one wife, as recounted by her husband: 'She'd stay in different flats … she'd come back at 2.00 am and go banging on the door to be let in. Drink had become a big problem for her … she set fire to our sitting room.'

An association between drink and infidelity occurs in the cases of five (50%) female excessive drinkers.[14] One woman was described by her husband as, 'drinking during the day … she might stay up until 3.00 or 4.00 am reading and drinking … she might go to a disco … [A man] was a regular caller to our house. I confronted her, she denied it.' The theme of general social failure recurs in several cases.

The gender of the excessive drinker does not appear to be significant in terms of the impact on the marriage. The only point of difference is that male excessive drinkers tended to be violent, whereas their female counterparts did not.

Both partners – excessive drinkers

In five marriages, both parties are described as excessive drinkers. One man stated that his drinking was in response to the problems created by his wife's alcohol abuse. In another marriage, the couple met while attending Alcoholics Anonymous. The man resumed drinking early in the marriage and breakdown followed. In another case, where both parties drank heavily, the man linked the pregnancy which precipitated the marriage with alcohol abuse: 'We hadn't a clue what we were doing ... drink featured far too much.'

The problems created by alcohol abuse are compounded when both parties are involved. Therefore breakdown is even more likely.

Response to excessive drinking in marriage

Spouses of excessive drinkers were faced with a crisis situation. Many responded by hoping that the situation would ameliorate. Some described the impact their spouses drinking had on them. A woman stated: 'I [was] eating ... and drinking too much ... I was absolutely degraded and humiliated.'

A man responded by withdrawing from the marriage. He stated: 'I was afraid to socialise with her ... I had no wish to make love to her. I could never have children by her ... I couldn't trust her.'

Many encouraged the excessive drinker to seek professional help. A wife stated: 'He went to [an alcohol treatment centre] ... he stayed off drink for six months. The rest of the year his drinking was very bad ... I persuaded him to go again ... seventeen times he received alcohol treatment.'

Some spouses issued ultimatums: 'I told her she would have to stay off drink or leave me.'

In all cases where alcohol abuse was a feature of the marriage, it is depicted in the tribunal files as a decisive factor in the destruction of the marital relationship and leading to separation.

Conclusion: Alcohol abuse

Alcohol abuse emerges as gravely detrimental to marriage. In some cases, the problem predated the marriage, while in others it commenced or worsened after marriage. There are frequent references to an association between intemperate drinking and problems such as infidelity, violence, deceit, distrust and ill-health. When both partners were heavy drinkers the effect was compounded. In some cases, excessive drinking is presented as a response to unhappiness in the marriage. Where present, alcohol abuse and related problems usually emerged as the principal reason for the failure of the marriage.

Gambling

Gambling is mentioned in eight cases which corresponds to 10% of our sample. In three cases, the gambling is not depicted as particularly serious. The wife in one of these marriages stated: 'The gambling did not effect me … but the drink affected me directly.'

In five cases gambling was a serious problem. In four marriages the problem resided with the man. In all five cases, gambling is associated with other problems, principally alcohol abuse, lack of companionship and financial irresponsibility.

Some men were very open about their gambling. One man stated: 'When I was married, [my gambling] got totally out of control … [My wife] might have gambled a little with me but no problem.'

A witness linked gambling addiction to financial problems and violence:

Most of his wages were gambled. She would come to me crying with bruises on her. He would have come to her looking for money and if he didn't get it, he hit her. They moved to rented accommodation but had to return to [her family] as the money was gone.

A link between gambling and other problems is common. Gambling and its financial implications placed major stress on the marriages affected.

There is impressive evidence of an association between an addiction to gambling and general social failure. Many gamblers experienced problems in work and several had alcohol problems. The impact on marriage was primarily in the financial sphere. However, it also effected the general relationship and created distrust between the couple. However, in the above cases, the spouses or witnesses do not reflect on the specific impact gambling has on marriage. Instead, they attributed the marital problems to broader social failure, of which gambling was but one feature. Therefore, it is not possible for us to draw precise conclusions regarding the role played by excessive gambling in the deterioration of the marital relationship. However, it is clear that it contributed in a substantial manner to the destabilisation of the marriages affected.

Drugs

Drug use is mentioned in four marriages, 5% of the total. In two cases, the level of use was negligible and could be characterised as experimentation. Of the other two couples, one spent their married life in Ireland and the other abroad. The Irish based wife stated:

> He had to have three or four joints at night ... unknown to me, it had been this way in courtship ... to enjoy a night out he needed a joint ... he [was] at wild parties, drugs involved and people hinted that infidelity was involved.

The husband admitted drug use but stated that his wife also took part.

Where present, drug use contributed to the unhappiness in the marriage and had profound implications for the couples' interpersonal relationship.

Drug use was a significant problem in two marriages in our study. In these two marriages, it is associated with a lack of confidence, misuse of alcohol, difficulties in relating with others and general irresponsibility. Drug use was but one of a number of factors that led to the breakdown of these marriage. However, our sub-sample is too small to permit general conclusions.

Conclusion

Alcohol, gambling and drink addictions had a gravely detrimental impact on the marriages concerned. Alcohol was the most common addiction and was linked to financial irresponsibility, infidelity and lack of companionship and, among men, with spousal abuse. Gambling usually occurred in conjunction with excessive drinking and impacted principally on the financial area. Both forms of abuse had a detrimental effect on the level of trust between the partners.

The number of marriages in which drug abuse was a significant factor is too small to permit sustainable conclusions. However, all three addictions were associated with general social failure and played a decisive role in the destruction of the marital relationship. These addictions destroyed the ability to interact with the other spouse and impeded the creation of a functioning relationship.

OTHER ISSUES IN MARRIAGE

Modern marriage emphasises the personal nature of the relationship and therefore is as varied as the couples who undertake the commitment. While we have covered the most common sources of destabilisation in our marriages, there remain several important factors that we have not adverted to. These include the continuation of a single lifestyle in marriage, class and educational factors, children, relations with the extended family, and the role of religion. In this final section we will analyse these factors.

Single lifestyle in marriage

Many of the marriages reviewed above were characterised by social failure on the part of one or other partner. Alcoholism, drug abuse, financial irresponsibility and violent behaviour are regarded as anti-social behaviour irrespective of the person's marital status. However, some marriages were not characterised by problems on this scale. These unions were undermined by one or other partner continuing to lead a single lifestyle in marriage. The person's behaviour *per se* was not the problem. The difficulty resided in the fact that the person behaved in a manner which is incompatible with marriage.

The continuation of a single lifestyle in marriage is most visible in the area of socialising. Even when alcohol abuse is not present, an inappropriate social life can frequently place a marriage under strain. In the case of a couple who married abroad a witness stated:

> [She] was discovering life for the first time ... she went haywire ... she started to stay out ... she discovered freedom. She is attractive and she had all these people paying compliments to her and simply didn't have the maturity to cope with the situation.

This woman left the marriage after becoming involved with another man. However, the witnesses regarded the couple's immaturity and the woman's social life as the cause of the breakdown and her meeting an alternative partner as merely the *coup de grace*.

This problem frequently took the form of a partner's refusal to assume responsibility. In the case of couples who married young there is often reference to one or other partner not being ready to 'settle down'. One wife stated: 'He was too young ... he always wanted to travel and he hadn't yet had the opportunity ... [He] just didn't want marriage.' Immaturity is the key element in these cases.

Virtually all marriages in our sample included elements of one or other partner continuing a single lifestyle in marriage. A failure to make the necessary adjustment is evident. The single lifestyle of his/her peers continued to be the dominant attraction and assumed greater importance than the relationship with the spouse. This tendency was more common among men that women. This may be due to women's greater involvement in caring for infant children.

Class/education differences

We saw in chapter two that there is little differentiation in terms of class and/or education between the partners to our marriages. However, class or education is mentioned as an issue in six cases. Social origin is mentioned in all six cases, while educational attainment occurs in two. In three cases, these factors are depicted as playing only a minor role in the deterioration of the marriage. In two cases, these issues are depicted as significant for the couples themselves. In a third case, differences in social background were an issue for the man's family of origin.

A typical case involved an unskilled worker and a woman in an administrative position. The husband did not co-operate with the tribunal. His wife, and the witnesses, detail his refusal to attend social functions concerning her job and his derisory references to her employment. Once again, this issue was relatively minor in the ranking of the marital problems. Lack of communication, alcohol abuse and infidelity emerged as the pivotal factors in the breadown of this marriage.

Educational and social class differences did not emerge as major issues in our study. The homogeneity within our marriages regarding these issues is the most likely explanation for this. In the few marriages where these issues are present, they appear to have played a contributory rather than a decisive role in the deterioration of the marriage. However, our sub-sample is too small to permit sustainable conclusions.

Children

Forty-seven (58.75%) couples in our study had children during their relationship. Sixty per cent of couples with children experienced either a premarital pregnancy or birth and most of the balance became parents within a short time after marriage. The birth of a child placed the relationship in a new context as new demands were made on the couple's time, money and emotional attention. Frequently, the arrival of children constituted an additional new source of tension and served to accentuate pre-existing problems in the marriage.

The presence of children did not effect both parents equally. Of the forty-seven mothers in our study, only fourteen (30%) are described as either drinking to excess or engaging in an inappropriate, extramarital relationship. This contrasts with an equivalent figure of 60% for men with children and 45% for women who did not have children. The presence of children had a more profound significant effect on the lifestyle of women than on that of men.

Marriages involving children tended to be of longer duration. The average duration of childless marriages in our study is 4.1 years, which contrasts with 7.6 years for marriages with children. There is evidence that the presence of children serves to increase the parents' determination to salvage the marriage. A mother stated: 'The only bright spot on the horizon was our child. He kept us together.' A woman cited her children as the reason why she returned to her violent, alcoholic husband: 'I went back ... because of the children.' However, the increased determination of one party to salvage the marriage for the sake of the children was rarely matched by the other party.

Paradoxically, children also placed the marriages under additional strain and exposed inadequacies in the relationship. This took many forms. In the case of a very young couple, the wife provided the following description of their reaction to the birth:

It was strange, we were little more than children ourselves and here we were with a baby. [He] was happy to have him and yet frightened to have him. We were both happy but confused.

The care of children was almost always exclusively assigned to the mother. In a typical case, the wife stated: '[My husband] wasn't a father to his child ... he was always gone.'

Occasionally, gender was an issue:

When [she] was born, he said 'I'd have gone home if I thought that it was going to be a girl' ... there was no excitement about her birth ... He never helped out and was indifferent about the whole thing.

Some saw children as a limitation on personal freedom. A father stated: 'I looked upon my daughter as a curtailment of my freedom.'

The same attitude was occasionally found among women. A wife stated: 'I was always trying to hand [the baby] over to my sister to mind.' A refusal or inability to accept the enhanced responsibility inherent in parenting is evident in all these cases.

In some families particular problems were present. One woman stated:

I had refused to have an abortion or adoption. So as [my husband] saw it, the responsibility was mine. He didn't want it. I don't think [my husband] ever changed [our child's] nappy... If [the baby] cried [he] couldn't handle it, he would walk out.

In the case of a child who suffered a prolonged illness, the witnesses indicated that the trauma involved exposed the inherent weaknesses in the relationship: 'Both [parents] were in the hospital for months on end ... neither of them were equipped to cope with this traumatic event.'

In some marriages the absence of children was an issue. A wife stated:

We were hoping to have children ... the doctor could see no

problem with me. [My husband] said he would, but he never had any tests done. ... he threw it in my face that I was childless. That really hurt me.

In this and similar cases, the breakdown of the marriage is not attributed to infertility but to problems such as alcohol abuse and lack of communication. The woman quoted above concluded by saying 'I believe alcoholism destroyed my marriage'. However, it is clear that the issue of children became a vehicle for the expression of the pre-existing problem in these marriages.

In a minority of cases, there is evidence of mistreatment or neglect of the children by one or both parents. In the worst example, the father served a prison sentence for physical abuse of the couple's infant child. There are no references to children of the couples in our study being victims of sexual abuse.

The decision whether or not to have children occasionally became a source of conflict. For one man it was the final straw in the marriage.

An unhappy marriage is frequently cited as a disincentive to having children. One woman stated that they didn't have children because: 'I wanted to sort out [my husband's] drinking problem first.'

The current view that having children is discretional rather than providential is reflected in our study. Unplanned pregnancies, even within marriage, are regarded as undesirable. Our subjects also see a stable relationship as a relevant consideration in the decision to conceive.

In conclusion, we note that the presence of children frequently served to accentuate pre-existing problems in marriage. Children brought new responsibilities and created additional stresses. A couple who do not have a satisfactory marriage are not well equipped to cope with this new challenge. Women were more likely than men to rise to the challenge. Children often constituted a barrier to separation; marriages with children had a longer average duration than childless ones.[15] A mother frequently remained in an unsatisfactory marriage for the sake of the children. Mothers attached particular importance to their children's safety; many who had endured violence over a prolonged period terminated the marriage when they felt their children were placed at risk.

Extended family

Relations with the extended family, principally in-laws, is mentioned as a problem in nineteen marriages. This represents 23.7% of the sample. In all cases, it was a relatively minor source of tension. This issue usually emerged as an allegation from one partner that his/her spouse was too involved with her/his family. Frequently, the complaint was expressed in terms of the amount of time that one partner spent with his/her parents. One woman stated: '[He] was very dependant on his family ... he would much prefer to go home to his own family for an evening meal ... I and [our child] would end up eating alone.'

A similar pattern is evident in other cases. One husband described his mother-in-law's role in the marriage as follows: 'It was indirect interference, coming up with ideas and [my wife] going along with it, either for us to be with them for dinner or suggesting that [she] buy this or that.'

Some attempted to explain why their family of origin continued to play such a big part in their lives. An unemployed husband provided the following rationalisation: 'I was never used to being alone ... With [my wife] working, I would go down home ... I couldn't stay on my own with [the child] in the flat.' The relationship with the extended family did not emerge as the major problem in this marriage.

Some subjects probe more deeply and see the relationship with the extended family as indicative of greater problems. Women frequently point to emotional factors. Many concluded that their husbands placed their family or mother foremost in their affections. In contrast, men usually concentrated on the influence exercised by her parents on his wife, rather than the focus of her affections. In these cases, while the role of the extended family was a considerable irritant, yet it was not regarded as instrumental in the breakdown of the marriages.

In many marriages where violence, infidelity or alcohol abuse were present the victim sought help from the extended family. Some resented their perceived inaction. A wife stated: 'They [my in-laws] knew there were problems. They did not want to know. They said he was my responsibility now.'

Many women received support from their own family. One woman stated: 'My mother was great. My sister went against him, once they knew he was hitting me.' However, her husband viewed the role played by her parents differently: '[She] used run to her parents a lot. It was more of a nuisance than anything else ... I'm sure her mother was telling her lots of things.' In these cases, the relationship with the family of origin is part of the effort by the victim to cope with distinct problems such as violence or alcohol abuse.

While our sample contains a multiplicity of quotations similar to the above, there is no evidence of the extended family playing a decisive role in the deterioration of a marriage. Some participants never adequately broke the link with their family of origin. This led to a lack of companionship in the marriage. In some abusive marriages, the victim sought help and solace from the extended family. Some saw the role played by the extended family as positive, while others saw it as undermining the marriage. These varying perceptions often occurred within the same marriage. However, in reviewing the evidence regarding the role played by the extended family, it appears likely that an element of *post factum* rationalisation is present. The bitterness created by separation frequently extends to the spouse's family. While the role played by the extended family was unhelpful in several cases, yet it is not of primary importance in explaining the deterioration of the marriage relationship.

Religion

In only one marriage was religion a major source of conflict. This marriage involved an Irish Catholic woman and a foreign born, nominal Protestant. A witness stated: 'He used the term hypocrite a lot. He opposed the children being brought up Catholic. Part of the reason was to put [his wife] down.' His wife viewed his lack of faith as a handicap in marriage: 'If [my husband] had a Christian belief, he might have found [marriage] easier ... He doesn't even believe that there is a God.' The issue of religion emerges as a manifestation of deeper problems in this marriage. Since there is only one case in this sub-sample, general conclusions are not possible.

CONCLUSION

Our analysis of the factors which served to undermine the marriages in our sample illustrates that the closer the link between a given factor and the couple's interpersonal relationship, the greater its impact on the marriage. Marriage is now centred on its core component: the quality of the marital relationship and particularly the satisfaction it brings to the participants. Anything which threatens this aspect of marriage places its survival in doubt.

Factors such as alcohol abuse, violence and infidelity served to undermine the quality of the couple's relationship. Emotional intimacy and trust, which are central to the current concept of marriage was negatively affected by these factors. Consequently, the satisfaction which the marriage brings to the partners is reduced. We found that the sexual relationship was frequently a barometer of the quality of the overall relationship. Problems in other aspects of the marriage were often reflected in the deterioration of the sexual relationship. This in turn led to a further deterioration in the broader relationship. Problems regarding money, accommodation or other tangible issues frequently acted in a similar manner. While these issues did not impinge on the core aspect of marriage, yet they served to accentuate pre-existing tensions. The presence of children had a dual, almost contradictory, impact on the marital relationship. The increased responsibility often exposed and amplified pre-existing inadequacies in the marriage. Paradoxically, children also served as a barrier and often led to the postponement of separation, since couples with children were less likely to accept the inevitability of separation. Issues such as class, educational differential and religion affected relatively few marriages. In the marriages concerned, they did not emerge as being of primary importance. While the absence of a control group is a handicap in the present study, yet the trends identified above serve to increase our understanding of broken marriages.

We saw in chapter three that our couples tended to marry without first establishing a close interpersonal relationship. Marriage, deprived of the social support which helped sustain it in the past, is now almost totally dependant on the quality of the interpersonal relationship. In our sample, the inadequacy of the couples' emotional unity was exposed by the various issues discussed in this section. The following or a similar phrase occurs is almost every case: 'There was no real communication in our marriage.' A failure or inability to communicate led to at least one spouse being dissatisfied with the meaning being derived from the relationship and is virtually a synonym for breakdown in the context of modern marriage. Many of the problems which were described by our couples as instrumental in the breakdown of their marriages, would most likely have been resolved in a well functioning marriage. This is particularly true of issues such as money, work, accommodation, sexual problems and relations with the extended family. Even more deep rooted problems such as alcoholism would be more likely to be overcome in the context of a close relationship between the couple. We saw that infidelity frequently was depicted as the result of the absence of such relationship or a reflection of another problems such as alcohol addiction.

Marriage stands or falls on the quality of the relationship and particularly the degree of personal happiness which it brings to the individual participants. The adjustment required is considerable and the active involvement of both partners in the negotiation of mutually satisfactory roles is necessary if the marriage is to succeed. However, many of our subjects, despite being married, failed to engage in this process and remained intolerant of anything which served to reduce their personal freedom. This lack of interaction resulted in a failure to adopt a lifestyle appropriate to marriage and parenthood. We noted that while this trend is more typical of men than women, it is common to both sexes. A second consequence of the increased emphasis on the individual is the reduced tolerance of unhappiness in marriage. In the Ireland of the 1950s participants in marriage, particularly women, were expected to endure whatever was entailed. Spouses who are dissatisfied with their marriages now have the option of leaving the relationship. In our next chapter we shall examine the circumstances under which our subjects chose to exit from marriage, how they effected separation, and how they coped with life after separation.

CHAPTER FIVE

Separation – What Went Wrong?

Chapter four outlined the various issues that were regarded by the members of our study as important in their marriages. Our most important finding was the central importance of companionship and emotional support within marriage. While problems regarding material matters such as work or money may place a marriage under stress, breakdown was usually caused by issues closer to the couple's interpersonal relationship. We found that a failure in effective communication and in the negotiation of satisfactory roles for each spouse is virtually synonymous with breakdown in today's understanding of marriage. In this chapter, we shall examine the transition from breakdown to separation. In the traditional concept of marriage, couples normally continued to cohabit almost irrespective of the quality of their marital relationship. Only in very rare cases involving extreme cruelty was separation contemplated and then only with great reluctance. Today, separation is more readily available and more frequently chosen. In this chapter, we shall reflect on the thesis that marital breakdown and separation is in essence a failure on the part of the couple to negotiate mutually acceptable roles within the marriage.

Commencement of breakdown

We saw in chapter two that the marriages in our study had an average duration of 6.2 years before the final separation occurred. However, a more significant factor may be the duration of the marriage as a satisfactory arrangement for the participants. Couples frequently continue to cohabit despite the presence of major problems in their marital relationship. The questionnaire used by the tribunal for petitioners and respondents contains a specific question regarding the duration of happiness in the marriage. In collating the replies to this question some difficulties arise. The partners may view the marriage differently and what may have constituted a satisfactory marriage for one partner may be regarded by the other as unsatisfactory. The term 'happy' is imprecise since the deterioration of a marriage is a process rather than a single event. Therefore, the identification of a precise point when the marriage ceased to be happy is difficult. In this study, we have followed the course of accepting the earliest date, as stated by one party. Once a marriage is perceived as unhappy by one participant, it has ceased to be satisfactory as understood by society generally. An additional problem consists in the unreliability of retrospective evaluation. The judgement of the parties as to when the marriage ceased to be happy may be coloured by negative experiences which occurred later. However, the testimony of witnesses helps counteract this factor.

The duration of happiness in the marriages in our sample ranged from never to seven years, the average being under a year (0.7 years). In thirty-four marriages (42.5%) at least one party regarded the marriage as being unhappy from the beginning.[1] These couples were typical of the broader sample, in terms of the length of courtship and the existence of pressures towards marriage such as premarital pregnancy. Surprisingly, they had a longer than average duration of marriage.[2] However, the marriages which are described as being unhappy from the beginning were also more likely to involve violence and sexual problems. In our total sample, 46.25% of marriages are depicted as violent while in the present sub-sample the figure is 58%. In the total sample 66.25% of couples experienced problems in their sexual relationship, which contrasts with 82% in the present sub-sample. In relation to problems such as alcohol abuse, infidelity or financial matters, there is no significant different between marriages described as unhappy from the beginning and the overall sample. Marriages depicted as unhappy from the beginning are less likely to involve children (32%) than the overall sample (41%).

An almost equally large group of marriages are those which are described as unhappy within the first year. This accounts for 33 cases (41.25%). The degree of differentiation from the overall sample is not pronounced. Consequently, it is not possible to relate the emergence of problems at such an early stage to any particular factor. Six marriages are depicted as becoming unhappy during their second year and three in their third year. The balance consists of one marriage which is described as being happy for four years, one for six years and the final marriage – seven years.

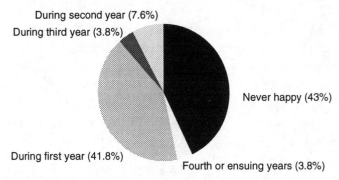

Figure 5.1 Duration of happiness in marriage

In summary, we have not succeeded in establishing an association between duration of happiness in marriage and any particular destabilising factor. It is likely that a selectivity factor is at work here. In our sample, 83.75% of marriages are depicted as either never being happy or as ceasing to be happy within the first year. This figure is unusually high when compared with other studies. O'Higgins in her 1974 study found that ⅓ of her subjects reported that her marriage went wrong from the beginning.[3] Ó Riagáin reports that among the clients of A.I.M. 60% believed that serious problems arose in their marriage within five years.[4] Nullity focuses on the validity of consent and therefore concentrates on the pre-marriage period and the early stage of marriage. Couples who depict their marriage as happy for a prolonged period are unlikely to see their application succeed. This skews our sample and renders conclusions regarding the commencement of breakdown in marriage untenable.

FACTORS ASSOCIATED WITH BREAKDOWN

We discussed in chapter four the role played by selected factors in marriage. In Figure 4.1 we presented the frequency with which various factors were present in our sample cases. We concluded that the closer the relationship that exists between a particular factor and the couple's interpersonal relationship, the greater will be the detrimental effect on the marriage. In this section, we will analyse in greater detail the association between the various factors. We shall isolate the marriages in which each factor was present and contrast these marriages with the complete sample.

Sexual problems were among the most frequently cited in our sample, occurring in fifty-three cases, 66% of the sample. Figure 5.2[5] contrasts the overall sample with the sub-sample of marriages which experienced sexual problems, in terms of the presence of other issues.

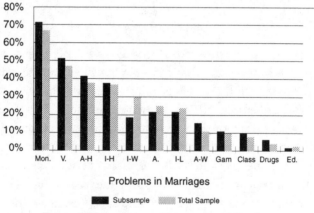

Problems in Marriages

■ Subsample ▒ Total Sample

Figure 5.2 Marriages with sexual problems

From Figure 5.2 it emerges that couples who encountered sexual problems in marriage were somewhat more likely to experience problems in areas such as finance, violence and alcohol abuse by both parties. However, the degree of differentiation is not pronounced. It is notable that no association emerged between sexual difficulties and infidelity. In fact, women in the sub-sample were less likely to be unfaithful. In chapter four we concluded that sexual

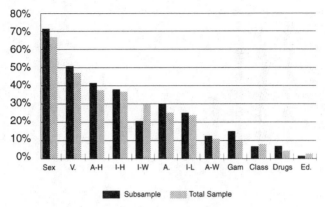

Figure 5.3 Marriages with financial problems

problems in marriage were usually a manifestation of other problems, principally the lack of a close affective bond. The sexual issue
tends to be a barometer of the overall well-being of the marriage
rather than a source of difficulty in its own right. Therefore the lack
of a distinctive profile in the present sub-sample is predictable.

Financial issues are another common source of difficulty. Fifty-
three cases included mention of financial problems. Figure 5.3 provides a comparison between this sub-sample and the overall sample.

An association between gambling and financial problems is
supported by Figure 5.3. In the total sample gambling occurred in
10% of cases and its incidence increases to 15% in this sub-sample.
The couples in our present sub-sample were somewhat more likely
to experience problems in terms of sexual issues, alcohol abuse by
both parties, accommodation, drug abuse, and violence. As in the
sexual area, the profile of the present sub-sample does not differ
significantly from the overall study. As discussed in chapter four,
financial difficulties also serve as a barometer issue. Couples in
well functioning marriages are likely to negotiate solutions to
financial problems without seriously damaging their relationship.
Insurmountable problems in dysfunctional marriages are likely to
be triggered by any problem area, including the financial. The real
problem is not so much the financial problem but the issue that
caused it and the couple's inability to negotiate a solution.

The next most common problem in our sample was violence

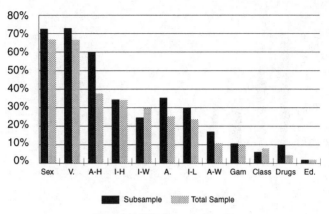

Figure 5.4 Violent marriages

which occurred in 46.25% of cases. Figure 5.4 compares this sub-sample with the total study and demonstrates that violent marriages are disproportionately prone to experiencing problems in almost all other areas. The only exceptions are female infidelity and problems based on class. The distinction between this sub-sample and the overall sample is particularly pronounced in the areas of male alcohol abuse and drug abuse. In this sub-sample alcohol abuse by husbands is mentioned in 59.4% of cases compared with 36.3% in the overall sample. The equivalent figures for drugs are 10.8% *versus* 3.75%. An association between violent behaviour and mood altering substances, such as alcohol and drugs, is widely documented and is supported by the present study. The destructive effect of violence on the marital relationship was discussed in chapter four.

Male alcohol abuse was a feature of twenty-nine marriages which represents 36.25% of the sample. Figure 5.5 analyses these marriages and demonstrates that marriages involving male alcohol abuse are significantly more likely to encounter problems concerning violence, sexual issues, finance, male infidelity and drug abuse. We have previously discussed the association between male alcohol abuse and spousal abuse. The link with infidelity is also striking. In the total sample, 35% of husbands are described as unfaithful; the equivalent figure in this sub-sample is 51%. The tangible

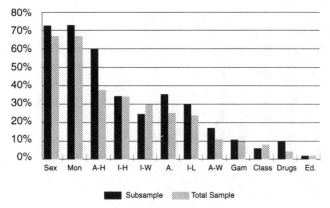

Figure 5.5 Alcohol abuse – husbands

effects of alcohol abuse are evident in the areas of money and accommodation. The incompatibility between alcohol abuse and a fulfilling marital relationship was documented in chapter four.

Female abuse of alcohol was a feature of just over 10% of marriages in the sample.

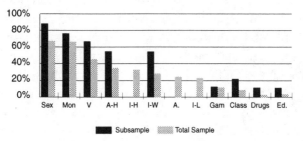

Figure 5.6 Alcohol abuse – wives

Figure 5.6 indicates a strong association between abuse of alcohol and infidelity among women. Female infidelity occurs in 30% of cases in the total sample and the percentage almost doubles (55.5%) when alcohol abuse is present. A context for the female abuse of alcohol may be provided by the fact that these women are more likely to have married men who also abused alcohol, and were violent, and to have experienced sexual and financial problems in marriage. However since this sub-sample consists of only nine cases, conclusions can only be drawn with caution.

Infidelity was identified in chapter four as constituting a major

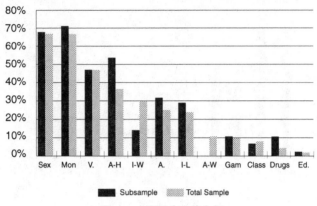

Figure 5.7 Male infidelity

crisis in marriage. Infidelity among males occurred in 35% of cases. Figure 5.7 summarises the relevant data. Male infidelity is associated with alcohol and drug abuse. In the total sample, male alcohol abuse occurred in 36% of marriages and drug abuse in 3.75%. Among the present sub-sample the corresponding figures are 53.5% and 10.7%. There does not appear to be an association between marital sexual problems and male infidelity. Men whose wives were unfaithful were less likely to be unfaithful themselves. The sample contained no example of a man, whose wife abused alcohol, being unfaithful. Though not included in Figure 5.7 the presence of children appears to be associated with a greater incidence of male infidelity. In childless marriages, 18% of husbands are described as unfaithful, which contrasts with 46% of fathers

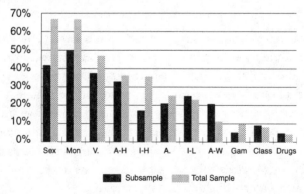

Figure 5.8 Female infidelity

who were unfaithful. An association between difficulties in assuming responsibility, and behaviour which serves to undermine the marriage, is evident here.

The context of female infidelity differs considerably from that of males. The only common factor is the role played by alcohol abuse. As depicted in Figure 5.8 marriages involving female infidelity were less likely to be subject to other problems. The presence of children had the opposite impact on women than men, i.e. women with children were less likely to be unfaithful than those who are childless. The relevant percentages are 25% and 36% respectively. We noted previously that female infidelity frequently took the form of a prolonged relationship that was likely to endure after the separation. In our sample, several such relationships were with previous boyfriends. In several cases, the woman's desire to pursue the 'alternative' relationship emerges as the only significant adverse factor in the marriage. The evidence suggests that, for women, both the positive features of the alternative relationship and the negative features of the marriage served to precipitate infidelity.

Conclusion

We have analysed the most important destabilising factors in the marriages in our sample. The remaining factors were either insignificant in terms of their impact on the marital relationship (viz. accommodation, education and class) or occurred too infrequently to permit a meaningful comparison with the overall sample (viz. drugs and gambling). In some cases, both limitations applied. Therefore, further analysis of our sample would be of limited value.

We have uncovered two categories of problem areas in marriage. One category can be termed barometer issues. These included sexual, financial and accommodation issues. Though significant in terms of impact in undermining the marriage, these issues were not the central problems in the marriage. Instead they reflected other difficulties, such as a lack of affection between the couple and an inability to negotiate solutions to problems. These issues appear significant because of their visibility but the real problem lies at a deeper level. Well functioning marriages would be likely to overcome challenges in these areas.

The second category of problems includes violence, alcohol/drug abuse and infidelity. These can be referred to as crisis issues since they strike directly at the essence of the marital relationship. It is likely that problems in these areas would place any marriage under considerable strain. The negotiation of a solution to these problems tests the unity, commitment and personal resourcefulness of the partners to any marriage. Our subjects were particularly unsuited to the task. For the most part, they entered marriage with a serious deficit in terms of preparation as individuals and as couples. Though frequently intimate on a physical level, our subjects were likely to be effective strangers on the level of emotions. The pressure generated by these problems exposed this inadequacy. As individuals, some coped better than others. There is considerable evidence of women being most likely to rise to the challenge of motherhood, marriage and homemaking. However, this distinction is not absolute. In all cases, even couples which included one party who apparently could cope with the challenges of marriage, the inadequacy of the other party and the superficial nature of the unifying bond make breakdown almost inevitable.

ATTEMPTS TO AVOID SEPARATION

All the members of our study stated or implied that they entered marriage hoping that it would bring happiness to both partners. All saw separation as undesirable. The efforts made by the couples to avoid separation varied considerably. Some separated after a relatively short time and appear to have made few efforts to salvage the marriage. In other cases, one or both parties made considerable efforts to avoid separation. This included staying in an unsatisfactory marriage for a long period in the hope that the situation would improve. This often resulted in a spouse tolerating inappropriate behaviour on the part of the other partner for an extended period. In this section we shall review the efforts made by the couples in our sample to avoid separation.

Strategies to avoid separation

Attempts to salvage the marriage usually centred on efforts to negotiate solutions to the problems in the relationship. Communication was a problem in every marriage in our study. Therefore, the efforts by the couple to solve their problems without outside help were always unlikely to succeed. This is reflected in the tribunal records. Comments such as 'all attempts at discussion provoked a row'; '[he/she] was never present long enough to allow fruitful discussion to take place'; and '[he/she] used promise me [he/she] would change, but never carried it through' are common-place. In a typical case, the wife stated: 'I don't think we had com-munication. If anything came up, it turned into a blow-up and he stormed out ... Nothing was ever talked out.'

A person who is unwilling or unable to engage in the process of negotiating solutions to problems in the relationship is unlikely to succeed in marriage as understood today.

Other couples adopted the strategy of temporary separations and some spouses imposed conditions prior to resuming cohabita-tion. One woman insisted that her husband see a psychologist as a condition for her agreement to resume cohabitation: 'I insisted that reconciliation would only take place if he did see someone first.'

Such commitments were not always honoured. Another wife stated: 'I asked him when we were separated [to attend coun-selling]. He would say yes, but when we were back together, he would not agree.'

In some cases, the casual nature of the premarital relationship re-manifested itself in the separation. One woman stated:

[During the second temporary separation we] just happened to meet and we spoke. We decided to come together again. One month later, I left him again. [His] drinking was only getting worse.

In a number of cases, the couple experienced several temporary separations and the final one became permanent: 'I left him not intending that it would be permanent ... I went back, but it only lasted two weeks ... He was not coming home ... He gave me hid-ings around the time when I left him and when I was back living with him.'

The strategy of temporary separations and efforts to persuade the other partner to avail of counselling displays a reluctance to separate. In these cases counselling was not likely to succeed since the partner only attended under duress, if at all. The commitment of one partner to the marriage was not matched by that of the other. Therefore, permanent separation was all but inevitable.

Involvement by intermediaries

A majority of couples sought help from counsellors or other professionals. In most cases the counselling was focused on the problems in the couple's relationships. However, in some cases, the original remit of the counselling was some other problem, such as alcohol abuse, and the focus was later broadened to include the marital problems. In our analysis, we have included all situations where at least one member of the couple discussed the problems in their marriage with a professional, even if the relationship was not the sole or primary focus. In this section, we shall include under the term 'counsellor or other professional', marriage counsellors, addiction counsellors, psychologists, medical doctors, social workers and priests.

In forty-seven cases (58.75%) at least one spouse discussed the marital problems, prior to separation, with a counsellor or other professional. In thirty-three cases (41.25%) both partners attended counselling. Women were more likely to avail of counselling than men. The relevant figures are forty-six women (57.5%) as opposed to thirty-four men (42.5%). In marriages where only one partner attended counselling, that party was more likely to be the woman. Our study includes thirteen cases in which the wife attended counselling alone, while in only one case the reverse occurred. As noted in chapter two, this suggests that women were more likely to seek help from counsellors, both for themselves and their partner.

Several couples failed to agree on the appropriateness of counselling to their situation. In many cases, the wife cited her husband's opposition as the reason why the couple did not seek counselling. One such woman stated: 'He wouldn't come with me [to a counsellor] so I didn't go either.'

Some families were opposed to the idea of counselling. A wife stated: 'He told me that counsellors were only scandalisers. His parents said counsellors were no use.' Some women sought help alone: 'I went myself to see [a priest]. He was the priest who married us. [My husband] did not come with me.'

Though less common, the reverse also occurred. Some men suggested counselling and their wives refused to attend. This occurred most frequently in situations where the wife had begun another relationship prior to separation.

Some couples differed on who to seek help from. A husband stated: 'It was my idea to talk to a priest; it was [her] idea that we see a counsellor. Our visits to these people made no difference; we knew what was wrong and what we had to do.'

In some marriages, one party now accepts that she/he was not committed to the future of the marriage and did not take counselling very seriously. One such man stated: 'We went to a marriage counsellor. I was not very co-operative. We went maybe four or five times. I can't remember the person's name.' These cases support the view that attendance at counselling with a reluctant attitude is likely to be a futile exercise.

Some subjects referred to their hesitation to talk to an outsider regarding personal problems. In one case, the woman stated: 'I talked to my mother, who used talk to a priest friend. I was very introverted and could not talk to anyone except my mother. I thought that I was in this for life and that it was my own fault.'

The idea of seeking professional help appears not to have occurred to some couples: 'I thought that we could sort it out ourselves. It was the last thing on my mind. I didn't know what to do.' The partners in these marriages frequently appeared to be mystified as to how to address the problems in their relationship.

The attendance of one partner at counselling alone proved futile. This is predictable, since in all cases the relationship was central to the problem. In addition, the person who refused to attend was frequently the person who was most lacking in the skills required in marriage.

In a small number of cases the advice offered by the counsellor is reported. In some cases, the professional concluded that there was no future for the marriage:

We went to see a priest and a counsellor. [The priest] advised us to go our separate ways. The counsellor couldn't give us any answers. She said that we knew ourselves what we had to do ... We said we would work at the marriage. We were afraid to follow [the priest's] advice.

In another case, the woman comments on the impact of the counselling: 'The counselling never really got off the ground. In the eight month separation, he did attend [a psychologist] ... His word was that [the psychologist] said that everything was fine.'

In these cases, the mammoth task required to salvage the marriage is manifest. Our couples did not prove equal to the challenge.

O'Higgins states that those of her subjects who consulted agencies only did so 'when the rupture was serious and very little could have been done'.[6] Many of our subjects were also reluctant to seek professional help. In most cases, the problems pre-dated the marriage and centred on the couples' failure to establish a close interpersonal relationship. Our couples would have been most likely to benefit from professional help *prior* to marriage. By the time marriage took place, the problems in the relationship were already profound and irretrievable breakdown was all but inevitable.

Conclusion

The skills required to negotiate a solution to the problems experienced by our couples are notably absent. Some couples attempted to resolve their problems without outside help, while others sought the help of counsellors or other professionals. Prior to marriage, they failed to establish a close interpersonal relationship. During the marriage the absence of emotional intimacy made coping with problems more difficult. Efforts to salvage the marriage were largely remedial efforts to create emotional intimacy. For some, personal problems, such as alcohol abuse, were an additional obstacle. Others lacked commitment to the marriage or the enhancement of the relationship. Some had already established an alternative relationship which he/she saw as preferable to the marriage.

The pattern of our couples being effective strangers on an emotional level is reflected in this section. When confronted with marital problems they did not have a reserve of trust and unity to call upon. Their superficial relationships were unable to survive the challenge constituted by the stresses of married life. Therefore, efforts to avoid separation consisted of attempts to create, rather than restore, a close interpersonal bond. What the couples should have accomplished in the more favourable circumstances of courtship, was now being attempted in the pressurised atmosphere, of a marital crisis. This proved to be a fruitless undertaking.

OCCASION OF SEPARATION

We previously noted that breakdown is not synonymous with separation. The vast majority of marriages in our study ceased to be regarded as happy by one or other party within a very short time. Yet in most cases, the couple continued to cohabit for a much longer period. During this period, efforts were usually made to retrieve the situation and avoid separation. In all cases separation required a decision by one party to cease living with the other. In this section, we shall examine the available data concerning the person who took this initiative and the circumstances of the final separation.

It is not always immediately obvious which party took the initiative regarding separation. A distinction between cause and occasion is relevant here. One party may leave the family home or eject his/her spouse. However, his/her action may be a response to unreasonable behaviour by the other partner which rendered continued cohabitation untenable. Since we have previously analysed the causes of separation, we shall now study the occasion. In the overwhelming majority of cases, the decisive initiative which brought about separation was taken by the woman.[7] In sixty-five cases (81.25%) the woman took the decisive action. In only ten cases (12.5%) did the man take this initiative. In five cases (6%) the separation was the result of a joint decision by the parties. Figure 5.9 presents this data.

Separation in the context of a new relationship

The circumstances of separation varied considerably. Some wives left the marriage in the context of having formed a relationship with a new partner. In one such case, the husband stated: 'She just threw

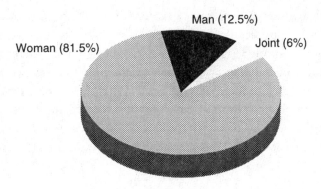

Figure 5.9 Initiative regarding separation

in the towel ... Within three weeks she was happy, seeing a psychologist and living with her new friend.' In these cases, the perceived attractions of the 'alternative' relationship proved to be a
major factor in causing separation.

The initiative was not always taken by the woman. In another case
the husband ejected his wife from the family home when he learned
that she had re-commenced a relationship with a previous boyfriend.
He stated: 'I packed her bags for her and sent her on her way.'

However, in most cases the initiative was taken by the person
who initiated the new relationship. Our sample also includes examples of husbands leaving the marriage in the context of being
involved in another relationship. One wife stated: '[He] decided to
make the break. His relationship with [his new partner] which went
on for some time before he left, was a factor.'

These situations are infrequent.

In these marriages a push-pull dynamic is at work. The perceived benefits to be derived from the new relationship contributed
to the creation of dissatisfaction with the marriage and the desire to
separate. Nevertheless most members of the sample were reluctant
to separate, either due to a concern for their children or a belief in
the permanency of marriage. Consequently, the establishment of a
new relationship placed the married person in a dilemma since the
marriage and the new relationship could not co-exist indefinitely.
In most cases the decision to pursue the alternative relationship

was made by the person directly involved. In a minority of cases, the other spouse short-circuited the process by ending the marriage. A comparison with a group who persisted in marriage after one partner formed an alternative relationship, would enhance our understanding of this process.

Separation in the other contexts

Not all separations occurred in the context of one or other partner opting to live with a new partner. Many women make an explicit link between their decision to leave and violence.

Many women in violent marriages had recourse to the legal system. One woman reacted to a particularly violent incident in the following manner:

> I was frantic … I didn't go back to him … I had got the police but they would not do anything while I was still with him. I had to go to court for a barring order. I started legal separation proceedings.

Some violent husbands terminated the marriage in abrupt fashion for no apparent reason. One woman stated: 'He threw me out and I went to my parents.'

In these cases, the decision to end the marriage was not premeditated. While many women in violent marriages contemplated separation in vague terms, the concrete decision to leave was frequently taken in a rushed manner in a crisis situation.

In other cases, the separation was not occasioned by a single incident but an accumulation of adverse factors. These adversities were frequently linked to alcohol abuse and/or infidelity. The following comment is typical of many: 'His drinking got worse ... he had been unfaithful ... We fought a lot and in the end I left him.'

Drink or infidelity were not always the key issues. Another wife depicted a lack of communication and affection as the principal problems in the marriage. In these cases the departing spouse is hesitant to leave the marriage. The decision to leave was taken reluctantly and gradually.

Some couples parted in amicable circumstances. One woman provided the following description of the separation:

My house wasn't ready so [my husband] and I continued to live under the same roof for a while even after getting the judicial separation.

These cases were exceptional. In most broken marriages an element of bitterness accompanied the final separation. We shall address this issue below.

Conclusion

The occasion of the final separation varied considerably. Several couples experienced one or more temporary separations prior to the final one. A male-female dichotomy is present here in that in most marriages the woman effected the final separation. We already noted that women were more likely than men to rise to the challenges inherent in marriage and parenthood. Women were also more likely than men to seek help from counsellors. The fact that women generally took the initiative regarding separation indicates that the women were frequently the discontented party in the marriage. This concurs with our earlier observation that women attach more importance to the emotive dimension of relationships, which was the missing element in most marriages in our sample .

NEW RELATIONSHIPS

Fifty-six men (70%) and fifty-two women (65%) are described as having formed new relationships. In thirty-eight marriages (43.75%) both parties entered subsequent relationships. These relationships varied considerably. Some had begun before the separation and were a causal factor in the ending of the marriage. Several were long-term, cohabiting relationships involving children. Many hoped to marry, if and when the option became available. Other participants were involved in several short-term relationships. Some characterised the new relationship in terms of friendship and were unsure of the future direction of the association.

The level of detail recorded in the tribunal records regarding second or subsequent relationships varies considerably. In some cases the existence of such a relationship is noted without comment. In other cases the person concerned, or a witness, comments on the stability of the second relationship. Due to the varying level of detail recorded it is not possible to compute accurate statistics regarding the duration of second relationships or the proportion involving cohabitation, children or a desire to marry.

No subject cited his/her status as married in the eyes of the church as a reason for not entering a new relationship. It is possible that some subjects who had not entered a new relationship held this belief but did not state it. One man protested his continuing belief in the validity of his marriage irrespective of any decision that the tribunal might reach. While he linked this belief with a decision not to marry, he did not express his intentions regarding other forms of relationships. A small number of women in new relationships referred to placing limitations on the relationship due to the non-marital nature of the association. Such limitations usually consisted of the exclusion of some or all of the following: sexual intimacy, cohabitation or having children. Some women referred to difficulties in meeting a suitable partner. Many linked this difficulty with a perception that separated women are sexually available. A similar perception did not appear to attach to separated men.

Some subjects stated their preference not to enter a new relationship. The reasons cited included a desire not to be 'hurt' again, a wish to concentrate on caring for their children, a fear that a new relationship would confuse their children and a belief that a person is happier alone. This approach is most common among women. Reflecting the fact that custody of children is usually assigned to the mother, only one man cited his children as his reason for not wishing to enter a new relationship. In these cases the application to the tribunal was usually motivated by a desire to close the chapter in the petitioner's life involving the unhappy marriage.

Relationships predating separation

Information regarding the commencement of subsequent relationships, as contained in the tribunal records, is frequently ambiguous. In many cases, the relationship was formed with a previous acquaintance or friend. This results in varying perceptions regarding the commencement of the relationship. The person involved may claim that, during the marriage, the relationship was on a platonic level and only later became affective. His/her spouse may view the matter differently and believe that the relationship prior to the separation was inappropriate. While it is not always easy to adjudicate such matters, the evidence of witnesses is helpful. In general, we have leaned towards seeing the relationship as beginning prior to separation, where there are indications that the other spouse saw it as a threat to the marriage.

Twenty-seven people (16.8%) entered into new relationships prior to separation. This breaks down as seventeen women (21.25%) and ten men (12.5%). The imbalance lends further support to our thesis that female infidelity in marriage is more likely to take the form of an ongoing relationship, which frequently endures after separation. Twenty-four marriages were characterised by one or other party beginning a new relationship prior to separation. In three marriages both spouses entered new relationships while still sharing the family home.

In all cases, the commencement of a new relationship is perceived as playing a major role in precipitating separation. In most cases, the partner involved linked the beginning of the new relationship to problems in the marriage. When asked to state what caused his marriage to break down, one such man stated: 'Total lack of communication, not seeing eye-to-eye on anything … [My wife was not] interested in the home or in me.' However, this relationship did not endure. The man stated: 'I have had a couple of relationships since the breakdown of the marriage.'

Women tended to enter more stable relationships. Regarding his wife, a man stated:

> She began an affair [with a man] who had left his wife and children. That was the end of our marriage. She is still living with [him] and they have one child.

However, not all relationships that predated separation proved stable. One woman is described as '[being] involved with someone else … She was involved with someone else after that and perhaps someone else again, I'm not sure.' As we shall discuss below, serial relationships are more typical of men than women.

Some relationships predated the marriage and endured after separation. A wife provided the following description:

Six to eight months before [marriage] I met another man ... we engaged in sexual relations ... We are still seeing each other [post separation]. It is still a sexual relationship. [My husband] did not know about him before the wedding.

In another case a man described how his wife 'had previously met [her present partner] ... She just told me one night, when we were in bed, that she was leaving me for him ... They are expecting another child.'

We have previously referred to the tendency of some unfaithful women to resume relationships during the marriage with previous boyfriends.

In some cases both parties had formed new relationships prior to separation. In one such case, the husband stated:

She told me that she loved him and she loved me but that wasn't possible. Neither of us would agree to move out. We were like two strangers. I also met someone else.

Relationships which began prior to or during the marriage were frequently the catalyst towards separation. Marriages involving spouses who had unresolved feelings for another person were placed under severe strain. The strain proved to be too much for our couples.

Unstable subsequent relationships

New relationships varied in terms of stability. Some resembled a marriage in all but official status. Others were depicted as superficial and as unlikely to endure.

Some participants became involved in a new relationship immediately after the separation. One women had the following experience:

I started another relationship quite quickly with a [man] who was separated from his wife. He gave me money for clothes and a great time. It became sexual ... It didn't work out.

The tribunal records also contain accounts of men becoming involved in short lived relationships immediately after separating from their wives.

Some witnesses expressed concern regarding the nature and stability of second relationships. In a report to the tribunal, a professional witness stated:

> [Her present partner] is too fond of drink, and can be violent to
> others but not to her, except on one occasion. When he is not
> drinking, he can be sensitive and caring. However, if he were
> married to her I am not sure he would act responsibly or kindly.

Some separated women became promiscuous or entered exploitative relationships. Speaking of a woman who was involved in
numerous relationships, a witness stated:

> One partner had a purely physical interest in [her] ... Another
> partner was very possessive. I feared for her safety and the chil-
> dren's safety. [We] had words about this ... I don't think that she
> was being paid as a prostitute but has been supported financially
> and has received material gifts.

Several men also conducted promiscuous lifestyles. However, in
such cases the descriptions tend to be shorter and do not include
expressions of concern. One man is described as having 'a son but is
not going out with the girl anymore. There were rumours of three
children, but I am only sure of one. He is a bit of a lad.'

Involvement in serial, superficial relationships appears to be a
manifestation of the trauma experienced by separated people in the
immediate post separation phase. Our study supports the contention that involvement in such relationships is frequently a temporary phase. However, a more detailed study conducted over a
number of years is necessary to permit definite conclusions.

The view that most promiscuous separated people engage in
this lifestyle for only a limited time is supported by the tribunal
records. Some subjects spoke of having found the 'perfect' partner
after a number of failed relationships. Though the person concerned may have misjudged the situation, it is probable that at least
some of these relationships are stable. Having described a long
number of superficial relationships, a witness stated that: 'There is
[now] a new person on the scene ... [he] seems a good person and is
a single person.' In describing her own situation, a woman stated: 'I

have had a couple of fairly short relationships. I am in a new relationship with a wonderful man who cares about me.'

A follow-up study of these subjects after an appropriate time-lapse would permit more definite conclusions. Our study is in the nature of a snap-shot of the present status of these relationships. However, the severe difficulties that many separated people have in forming new relationships is evident from the cases reviewed above.

Stable subsequent relationships

Many applicants to the tribunal were involved in stable relationships which they believed would endure. Some such relationships involved cohabitation, children or civil marriage.

Many participants speak of having a 'friend' who helped them cope with the trauma of separation. A woman's perception of negative attitudes towards separated women is evident in this quotation:

Things have worked out really well. I have a steady fulltime job … I didn't want to go out at first. I felt that people were talking. Now I love my day off. I have a good companion and we just meet socially once a week. He is very like my dad, he has the same qualities.

A witness reflected on the positive impact of the new relationship on the woman concerned: 'She has her life together and she is involved in a new relationship and I have never seen her as good as she is now. She is taking pride in herself … She was at an all time low but she has rounded the corner.'

This woman's need for affirmation and affection is typical of many female subjects. The role played by her companion appears to have been primarily in the area of enhancing her self-image. While men are less likely to speak in these terms, the tribunal files contain examples of some men having similar experiences:

Three years after leaving [my wife] I met [my present partner] … we are still together ... we have a beautiful [child] … Without [my partner's] love, I don't believe that I would be as happy and content as I am now.

In these cases, the new relationship played a major role in helping the person concerned cope with the breakdown of the marriage.

Marriage was not envisaged in all cases. Some subjects stated that though their present relationship was stable they believed that marriage would not ensue, even if the option became available: 'I have a boyfriend, but I do not foresee that it will lead to marriage.'

Such applications to the tribunal are frequently motivated by a desire on the part of the petitioner to close the chapter in his/her life involving the unhappy marriage. Due to their experience of unhappiness in marriage, many separated people are reluctant to make a similar commitment to a new partner. However, in situations where a decree of nullity is granted many undergo a change in attitude and do actually marry.

Conclusion

The disparate nature of the new relationships established by our subjects is their most obvious feature. Those that pre-dated marriage were most likely to be stable and frequently involved cohabitation and the presence of children. The most stable relationships resembled marriages in all but official status and the application to the tribunal was usually motivated by a desire to validate this union through marriage in church. Several members of the study became involved in relationships which, despite not enduring, were not exploitative. Others adopted promiscuous lifestyles and engaged in serial, superficial sexual relationships. While men were more likely to adopt this lifestyle, there was also a high proportion of women involved. Some of these relationships were exploitative and constituted a risk to the physical well-being of the woman concerned and her children, where present. For many participants the adoption of this lifestyle was linked to the traumatic nature of marital breakdown. For most there is evidence that the conclusion of this phase was occasioned by the commencement of a supportive relationship. However, in evaluating our findings, it is important to remember that our study is akin to a snap-shot. The situation of many of our subjects may change dramatically in future years.

Our study suggests that separated people find the establishment of new relationships particularly difficult. The group who coped best were those who had a ready-made alternative relationship available. In such cases, the difficulties inherent in separation was eased by the support of the 'alternative' partner. Others experienced social failure and personal problems on a broad scale and found the establishment of a stable relationship difficult. Some stated their determination never to become involved in an intimate relationship again.

IMPACT OF BREAKDOWN ON INDIVIDUALS

The tribunal records contain considerable evidence of the trauma inherent in marital separation. Sometimes the experience of marriage itself was the primary source of the trauma; in these cases, separation is often seen as a relief. Other participants depict the actions of their partners, and in particular the events surrounding the separation, as a betrayal and find it difficult to cope with the ending of the marriage. In this section we shall review the available evidence regarding these issues.

Impact of separation

The impact of marriage breakdown and separation appears to be greatest in the case of women. The impact included symptoms such as lack of self-confidence, psychological and general ill-health, and an aversion to becoming involved in a new relationship. One woman provided the following description: 'I have been seeing [my husband] everywhere; coming out of the jamb of the door even. I have to carry valium.' In another case, a witness provided a similar description: '[She] went through a very traumatic time ... she was very hurt and very traumatised ... she went to see a counsellor hoping to be able to come to terms with the fact that the marriage was over.'

While the cases quoted here are at the extreme end of the spectrum, most women in our study referred to suffering some aftereffects of an unhappy marriage. The exceptions are those women whose marriages were relatively happy but who opted to pursue a relationship with another partner.

While women are more likely to refer to the pain of separation, the tribunal files also contain accounts by men. One man stated:

I have no new relationship. I have discovered the pain, hurt, isolation on my own ... I live in hope that some day I can fulfil my dreams again ... for the first time I understand why people commit suicide ... it frightened me. The marriage took a terrible toll on me, physically, mentally and emotionally.

In a more typical, less traumatic case a witness described her brother's difficulty in coping with separation and his lingering antagonism towards women: 'He seemed to be without direction ... He is bitter towards [his wife] and women in general ... he is not ready for marriage.'

We previously noted that women appear to attach more importance to the emotive aspects of marriage. Perhaps reflecting this fact, men coped differently with separation. However, in situations where the man found the experience traumatic, the symptoms experienced resembled those undergone by women. The infrequency of references to men suffering trauma raises the question of how men coped with marriage breakdown.

While accounts regarding men are less likely to contain references to mental angst, there is evidence in many cases of social failure and personal problems.[8] Frequently, there is evidence that the problems which had served to undermine the marriage persisted. This is especially likely in the case of alcohol abuse. A witness stated:

[He] hasn't changed at all ... drinking most of the time ... He moved in with his parents ... he has no interest in any other woman. He shows no interest in the children and ... he doesn't support them.

A new relationship did not always prove to be a panacea: '[He] is in a new relationship. He has got into a lot of trouble with the police as a result of drink ... He has got very mixed up.'

It is evident that for many men the problems which prevented them from succeeding in marriage continued post-separation. For some, the situation deteriorated further once the positive influence exercised by their wives was removed. Men experiencing such problems were unlikely to engage in much self-reflection and therefore the lack of references to emotional factors in their evidence becomes intelligible.

A male-female dichotomy is evident in how our subjects coped with separation. An emotional, traumatic response was more typical of women. Men, by contrast, were more likely to take solace in drink. It is likely that the emotions experienced by both sexes were similar, though the mode of expressing and coping with the trauma varied greatly.

Family, counselling and professional help

Separated people frequently sought help from family, friends, counsellors and professionals. A separated woman's sister told the tribunal: '[She] is dwelling too much on what went wrong ... but for my parents and the support that they are giving her, I think that she would find it very hard to manage ... she's drinking a good deal as well.'

Others availed of programmes such as B.E.[9] One such woman stated: 'I have built up my trust and confidence. I have been involved in B.E. I am seeing a Psychiatrist, on a regular basis.' Professional help was not always successful. A man stated: 'I had a long chat with [a priest] and he advised me to see a counsellor which I'm doing. I had joined B.E. but it did not do the trick for me.'

The support of family, friends and counsellors proved to be positive in most cases. Women were more likely than men to seek and to be open to professional and other help. The available detail is insufficient however to allow more detailed conclusions.

New relationships

We have already discussed the positive impact of a new relationship on the process of coping with separation.[10] However, in several cases there are indications that, having experienced an unhappy marriage, some participants are reluctant to become involved in a new relationship. One witness attested to her sister's resilience but added that the after-effects of the marriage are still present:

[She] has regained a lot of her self confidence... Her health is much improved. She has a wide circle of friends. She is involved in support groups ... she has built up a good life for herself ... She has moments when she would lapse back to memories of the past ... she is very wary of getting involved in a new relationship.

The theme of women's reluctance to become involved in a new relationship occurs in several cases.

Some men had similar feelings. A man who has custody of the children states: 'I am managing fine with the children. I do not see myself re-marrying, definitely not in the near future.'

We have previously discussed the difficulty which many separated people had in meeting an acceptable partner.

A reluctance to enter a new relationship was most common among women who had experienced violent or traumatic marriages. However, this aversion was also found among other categories of participants. Some subjects refer to being opposed to entering a new relationship initially and then undergoing a change in attitude. This was usually occasioned by the option of a new relationship, in the concrete form of meeting a prospective new partner. It took many subjects a considerable time to accept such a relationship, though for most it proved a substantial help in overcoming separation. However, a reticence regarding new relationships is established in our study as a possible consequence of marriage breakdown.

Negotiating separation

An important factor in life after separation is the nature of the agreement made with the former spouse. The key points at issue are custody of and access to children, money and property. The tribunal records include information regarding arrangements concerning children, property and maintenance in seventy-three cases. The level of detail varies enormously. In some cases the records simply state that an agreement was reached. In other cases, details of the agreement are listed. The Tribunal records indicate that nine couples (12.3%) received a civil divorce abroad[11] and two couples (2.7%) received civil annulments from the Irish High Court.

In forty-four cases, the couples refer to approaching the courts or a solicitor regarding family law issues other than divorce or civil annulment. These cases are difficult to classify, since the parties do not always clearly state which aspect of family law they had recourse to. It is likely that several of these cases consisted only of a consultation with a solicitor and that many did not reach court. However, we can state that our sample does not contradict the findings of Fahey and Lyons regarding the two-tier nature of Irish Family Law.[12]

In fifteen cases, there are references to no formal agreement being reached regarding children or property. In many of these cases, the couple ceased to have any contact and/or one party (usually the man) moved a considerable distance away. Some couples managed to reach an amicable agreement, without recourse to the legal system. Several couples did not have children or joint property and therefore a formal agreement was unnecessary. Reflecting the limited availability of the service in the West of Ireland, there is no reference in our sample to the involvement of a mediator.

Many couples provided details of the arrangements agreed regarding children and the family home. Forty-seven couples had children and it is possible to establish in forty-one cases the arrangements reached regarding custody or access. In the vast majority of cases (80.4%) the woman has sole custody of the children. In a further two cases (4.8%) the couple had joint custody. In six cases (14.6%) the man had sole custody. Our findings regarding the residence of children are in broad agreement with the findings of Fahey and Lyons and Ward.[13] Figure 5.10 presents our data on this topic.[14]

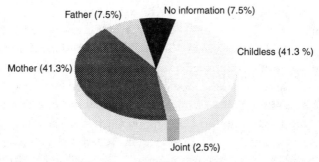

Figure 5.10 Custody of children

In all cases where the man had sole custody, the woman began another relationship during the marriage and eloped (without her children) with her new companion. In two cases, the woman later sought custody of the children in court. In the remaining four cases, the woman did not seek custody. The husband in one such case described how custody was awarded to him in court:

The psychologist gave a bad report about her to the court. He said that she was not fit to be a mother ... I gave her some money and she went back to join her boyfriend ... [She] has access to the kids.

Five non-custodial mothers exercised their right of access to the children. The sixth woman lives abroad with her new partner, and has no contact with her children. In her interview she stated that she is resigned to this situation. Three mothers who did not have custody of their children are described as suffering from severe personality and/or addiction problems. The general pattern of the woman having custody of the children, except where there are exceptional circumstances, is confirmed in our study.

Information concerning access by the non-custodial parent is recorded in thirty-seven cases. In the majority of cases (67.5%) the other parent exercised his/her right of access. The remaining twelve non-custodial parents did not have any contact with their children and frequently lived abroad or elsewhere in Ireland. Female, non custodial parents were more likely to exercise access than their male counterparts. The contrasting percentages are 83% for women and 55% for men. With one exception all mothers had either custody of or access to their children. By contrast eleven fathers had no regular contact with their children.

Information concerning possession of the family home after separation is difficult to access. Several couples had lived in rented or local authority accommodation and consequently the question of ownership did not arise. Some couples sold the family home when they separated. Some couples lived abroad and one or both partners returned home post-separation. In twenty six cases, the tribunal files contain definite indications regarding the possession of the family home. Nineteen women (73%) and seven men (26.9%)

retained possession of the family home. These percentages are in broad agreement with those presented by Fahey and Lyons.[15] In cases where the man retained possession of the family home, the house concerned was frequently connected with the ancestral family farm or business or the wife had chosen to depart. Our information regarding the payment of maintenance or a financial settlement is not sufficient to permit meaningful analysis.

Relationship between the couple

While accurate determination of matters as nebulous as relationships between people is impossible, yet it is feasible to assign the ongoing relationship of each couple in the study to one of three groups: no relationship, hostile or cordial. Based on an approximate categorisation of our cases, the post-separation relationship of fourteen (17.5%) couples can be described as cordial, forty-three couples (53.75%) as hostile, while the balance, twenty-three couples (28.75%), had no contact at all. In this section, we shall review each group and seek to elucidate the factors which influence the couple's post-separation relationship. This information is presented in Figure 5.11.

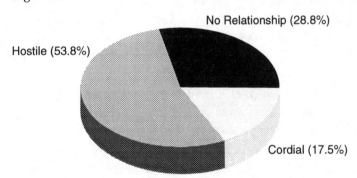

Figure 5.11 Post-separation relationship

Couples with a cordial post-separation relationships were less likely to have had a particularly traumatic marriage or separation. Of the fourteen marriages concerned, 35% were characterised by violence, which compares with 46% for the total study. Reference to individual cases helps elucidate the reality behind the figures.

Some couples continue a cordial relationship and there is evidence of ongoing friendship and social contact. One husband stated: 'Whenever I call, she gives me a cup of tea ... I was there for Christmas Day, the kids were with me for five days, after it.' Another man expresses his wish to continue an amicable relationship: 'I want to be her friend at least.'

A small number of respondents reiterated their belief in the validity of their marriage. One husband stated:

> I married my wife in good faith. I had children by her. I consider our marriage to have been a valid marriage ... Should a decree of nullity be granted ... I will not ever re-marry.

It is likely that this view is shared by some respondents who opted not to co-operate in the tribunal investigation.

Twenty-three couples (28.8%) are characterised as having no relationship post-separation. This frequently occurred in the context of the partners living a considerable distance apart. It is notable that these couples were less likely than average to have had children (sub-sample: 26%, total study: 58.75%). The absence of a common link such as children makes interaction less necessary. These marriages also tended to be somewhat shorter than average (5.2 years as opposed to 6.2 years). In one such case, the wife described the couple's present relationship as follows: 'I know nothing about him. I've no contact with him, even at Christmas.'

The absence of contact may be due to its lack of necessity, e.g. in the case of childless couples. Alternatively, it may reflect logistical problems, often distance, acrimony or problems such as alcoholism.

The largest group is the forty-three couples (53.75%) whose present relationship can be characterised as hostile. This hostility can arise from several sources. Children are frequently the vehicle for the expression of the ongoing bitterness.

In these cases, the bitterness is expressed in reduced co-operation regarding access to children, threats to prevent future access, rows over maintenance and the occasional exchange of insults. However, though not involving violence these tensions contribute significantly to the creation of unhappiness in the lives of all concerned.

In some relationships the aggression which had characterised the marriage continued post-separation.[16] Many victims continued to fear their husbands: 'I'm still afraid of him.' Some separated wives plan to go abroad to escape their husband's harassment: 'I'm nervous of him. I'm leaving this summer. I would like to get away myself and get [my son] away from his father's influence.' Others sought the protection of the courts and the Gardaí: 'He broke in and stole my money. He threw condoms on the door step. He followed us with a knife and threatened to take the children. I got the Gardaí to talk to him ... I have a barring order, *sine die.*'

For these couples, the problems which undermined the marriage continued to poison the relationship after separation. Many women had recourse to the Gardaí or the courts, while others moved residence. The extreme antipathy which characterised some post-separation relationships was frequently a temporary phenomenon. In many cases, once the initial bitterness subsided, the relationship improved. Other hostile partners entered a new relationship and their feelings mellowed.

Over half our couples had an unsatisfactory relationship after marriage. In several cases the problems which undermined the marriage continued to impair the relationship after the separation. This was particularly true of marriages involving violence, antisocial behaviour or alcohol abuse. Couples who were obliged to have contact, usually due to the presence of children, tended to experience most difficulty. Perhaps it is not altogether surprising that couples who failed to negotiate satisfactory roles in marriage, also failed to negotiate a mutually satisfactory relationship after marriage. Many women sought legal protection or moved residence to avoid these problems. Over a quarter of our couples had no relationship after separation. These couples were less likely than average to have had children and frequently lived a considerable distance apart. The remainder of our sample had a generally satisfactory relationship. These marriages and separations tended to be less traumatic than the overall sample.

CONCLUSION

Before reaching general conclusions, it is important to consider the nature of our sample. Nullity consists in defective consent to marriage. Applications concerning marriages which ended due to a moral failure or the deliberate decision of one or other spouse rarely proceed past the initial stage. Therefore, it is likely that significant categories of broken marriages are not included in our study. There are a considerable number of people, many of whom are Catholics, who choose not to apply to the tribunal. However, as previously discussed, the non-availability of civil divorce served to reduce the impact of the latter factor. Despite these limitations, we can identify three groups of separated spouses – the resilient, the traumatised and the drifters.

The first group is characterised by resilience. They coped best with separation. Most had played a constructive role in the marriage and its failure was usually due to the lack of commitment and/or the inappropriate lifestyle of the other partner. There is considerable evidence of mature personal traits in this group. Some had entered marriage in less than ideal circumstances; such as premarital pregnancy. However, most saw separation as a last resort and devoted considerable effort to saving the marriage. However, all had reluctantly come to accept separation as the only option. This group is proactive and usually had taken the initiative that led to separation. Members of this group usually had custody of the children. Many had entered a new relationship since separation and wished to marry his/her new partner. While women were in the majority in this group, there was also a significant minority of men.

The second group can be characterised as traumatised. Again women are in the majority. This group tended to be more passive and had endured inappropriate behaviour by their partners over a long period. Members tended to have had violent, unfaithful, excessive drinking or financially irresponsible spouses. This group generally responded by hoping that things would change. Separation usually occurred when the other partner initiated it, or the situation reached a climax. Some continued to be harassed by the other partner even after separation. This group coped poorly with separation. Many needed professional help and most had reservations about entering a new relationship. Despite frequently having custody of the children, most depended on family or friends for their own emotional survival. Some members of this group had not overcome the trauma at the time of their interview by the Tribunal. However, most had learned to survive through the help of family, friends, counsellors, support groups, or in many cases, a new partner.

Our third group is characterised by drift. They were relatively unaffected by the ending of the marriage. This group was dominated by men, though a significant minority of women are also included. In some marriages, both partners could be assigned to this group. They conducted a lifestyle which is inconsistent with a committed relationship during marriage and continued to do so after the separation. Most drifted into marriage and made little effort to ensure its success. Drift also characterised their disengagement from the marriage. Lack of commitment, alcohol abuse and an openness to casual sexual relationships characterise this group. Marriage had very little impact on them. Few had custody of the children and most did not avail of access to their children. This group was the least likely to co-operate with the tribunal. For the most part, we are dependant on the testimony of the other party and witnesses for information regarding members of this group. There is overwhelming evidence of immature personal traits in this group.

In all cases, separation was a major event in the lives of the people concerned. The time lag between the cessation of happiness in the marriage and the advent of separation is indicative of its undesirability from the point of view of most members of the sample. The marriages in our sample are characterised by a failure in negotiation of roles. As we saw in chapter one, the impersonal norms of the past are no longer accepted as adequate. Participants in marriage now demand a much closer emotional involvement and a greater sharing of all aspects of life. We found in our study that women were more likely than men to embrace this vision of marriage on a practical level. This concurs with the findings of Hannan and others.[17] Women are more likely than men to be dissatisfied with marriage and take steps to effect separation. However, in most cases their decision to separate was a reaction to what they regarded as the unsatisfactory role played by the husband in building a true partnership. In most cases considerable efforts were made to avoid separation. These consisted in attempts to discuss the problem in the marriage with or without the aid of outside help. However, the failure to establish a close interpersonal relationship in the less pressurised context of courtship, combined with a lack of practical commitment by one or other partner, rendered these attempts futile.

CHAPTER SIX

Where Do We Go From Here?

A sociologist made the following comment regarding the present state of our knowledge concerning marriage breakdown in Ireland:

> It is almost incredible that we know comparatively little about the social characteristics of those who are withdrawing from marriage and/or being deserted.[1]

The purpose of the present study is to use a heretofore untapped source of information to address this gap in our knowledge.

SUMMARY OF CONCLUSIONS

Family of origin

In our analysis of premarital factors, the influence of the family of origin emerged as extremely important. We found that the absence of a model of a functioning family during formative years severely impaired the ability to cope with marriage in adult life. Many of the skills needed in marriage, specifically those concerned with compromise and negotiation, appear to be learnt at an early stage in the family of origin. Most of the members of our sample were lacking in these skills. People whose families of origin were characterised by violence, alcohol abuse, infidelity by a parent or the absence of affection, experienced special difficulties in coping with adult intimate relationships, specifically marriage. We found that the role of the mother was more significant than that of the father. This reflects the persistence of female dominance in the socialisation of the young.

Previous relationships

An enduring attachment towards a previous girl/boyfriend was a destabilising factor in some courtships and marriages. Indecision regarding which partner to select for marriage served to dilute the individual's commitment to the marriage and consequently served to destabilise the marital relationship. Women who were caring for a child from a previous relationship emerged as being prone to making ill-advised decisions regarding marriage. These mothers frequently believed that the choice of potential marriage partners available to them was limited and consequently made hasty and ill-advised decisions regarding marriage.

Courtship

The members of our sample married people who resembled themselves in relation to tangible matters such as age, social class, religion and wealth. However, in many marriages there was considerable divergence within the couples when concept of marriage and ability to undertake the role of spouse are considered. The explanation for this anomaly is likely to centre on the fact that most of our couples married without effectively exercising deliberative thought. The decision to marry was frequently made in the context of a pressure such as a pre-marital pregnancy and the focus shifted from a decision regarding marriage to crisis management. Marriage became a strategy, rather than a goal in itself. In some courtships, the dominant characteristic was 'drift' and involved almost imperceptible movement from friendship to an exclusive relationship, to sexual involvement, occasionally to cohabitation, to engagement and finally to marriage. A form of marriage dependant on interpersonal union was always at risk due to the failure to create a close interpersonal union in courtship.

On a descriptive level, we noted that sexual involvement is increasingly becoming a standard part of the premarital experience for Irish couples. The previous sequence of marriage, sexual involvement and conception is rapidly receding. A new sequence that places sexual involvement, occasionally conception, and increasingly frequently cohabitation before marriage is on the ascendant. Their courtships also demonstrate that attitudes towards sexual involvement are characterised by a new liberalism.

However this liberalism is not all embracing; abortion still carries moral overtones and cohabitation was largely confined to couples living away from home. While sexual activity outside of marriage was accepted by most couples, conception or childbearing was less acceptable. There is also evidence of a divergence between the generations in their views regarding appropriate sexual intimacy before marriage. Many couples expressed their own acceptance of cohabitation and/or child bearing outside of marriage, yet most referred to familiar and social pressures as propelling them towards marriage.

Formal preparation for marriage

The comments of the members of our sample regarding their experience of formal preparation for marriage were predominantly negative. The focus on tangible issues such as budgeting was especially criticised. An alternative concentration on relationships and conflict resolution was favoured by most. Many subjects recognised that their own disposition at the time of marriage also mitigated against the success of premarital preparation.

Issues in marriage

In reviewing the issues which undermined the marriages in our sample, we identified some factors as 'Barometer Issues'. Such issues included sexual[2], financial, and accommodation problems. These were an expression, rather than the root cause, of the unhappiness in the marriage. A functioning marriage would most likely overcome problems in these areas.

We used the term 'Crisis Issues' to indicate problem areas that would place any marriage, irrespective of how well it had functioned heretofore, under strain. These issues included alcohol or drug abuse, excessive gambling, violence and infidelity. Problems in these areas disrupted the couple's relationship and placed the future of the marriage in doubt. Our couples, due to their failure to establish a close interpersonal relationship in courtship, lacked the emotionally supportive bonds necessary to carry their marriages through these crises. We concluded that the closer a problem is to the couple's interpersonal relationship, the greater is the impact on the marriage.

Separation

Most of our subjects did not choose separation flippantly. This is evident from the time-lag between the end of happiness in the marriage and separation occurring. Factors such as commitment to marriage as a permanent union, a desire to remain in the marriage for the sake of the children, lack of confidence, or lack of an alternative, frequently served to delay separation. In most cases, a catalyst was required to provoke separation. Possible catalysts included: the instigator of separation beginning a new relationship or suffering an unacceptable level of violence; the children becoming exposed to the risk of violence; or a spouse becoming convinced that the problems in the relationship would not ameliorate. A new relationship often created a new comparison level for alternatives to the marriage and facilitated separation.

Coping with separation

We identified three dominant groups among the separated. The first was characterised by resilience and they coped best. Most had played a constructive role in the marriage and its failure was usually due to the lack of commitment and/or the inappropriate lifestyle of the other partner. Members of this group usually had custody of the children, many had entered a new relationship and wished to marry their new partner. Women were in the majority in this group though it also included a significant minority of men.

The second group are distinguished by being traumatised. This group was rather passive and had endured inappropriate behaviour by his/her partner over a long period. Some continued to be harassed by the other partner, even after separation. Despite frequently having custody of the children, most depended on family, friends, a new partner or professionals for their own emotional survival.

The third group is characterised by drift. They were relatively unaffected by the marriage or by the separation. They conducted a lifestyle inconsistent with a committed relationship during the marriage and continued to do so after the separation. Men were in the majority in this group, few had custody of the children and most did not avail of access to children. Most members of this group have personal problems, frequently alcohol abuse.

Gender differentiation

We uncovered considerable gender differentiation in our review of the marriages in our study. In general, women were more likely than men to rise to the challenge of marriage and make appropriate adjustments to their lifestyle. They were also more involved in the caring for children and in assuming responsibility for the home. Women attached more importance to the emotional aspect of marriage; this was especially notable in the sexual area. Men persisted in a more detached view of marriage and were more likely to focus on material issues. Women were more proactive in recognising problems in marriage, in seeking to address them and, once they became convinced that these efforts were futile, acting to effect separation. Women who were unfaithful during marriage were more likely to become involved in relationships involving a high level of emotional investment, which frequently endured after separation. Post-separation women were in the majority in the groups which we have characterised as resilient and traumatised. Men were more likely to persist in the lifestyle which had contributed to the undermining of the marriage.

Continuity and change

A constant theme of this study, and recent sociological literature on marriage in Ireland, is change. However, in chronicling this change there is a danger of overlooking the elements of continuity that persist. Stereotyping is always a danger: marriage in the past was not totally devoid of an affective element and present day marriages are not insulated from economic or other material influences or from broader cultural norms.

We used the seminal research undertaken by Arensberg and Kimball in 1930s Ireland as the backdrop to the present study.

There are numerous points of contrast between the approach to marriage described by these authors and that portrayed in the present study. However, there is also ample evidence of continuity. People from similar backgrounds continue to marry each other. Marriage is still seen as having a religious dimension; despite a drop in regular church attendance almost all couples still opt for a religious form of marriage. Marriage continues to be seen as a monogamous relationship. Though more common than in the past, infidelity is still regarded as inconsistent with marriage. There is little evidence of a divorce mentality among our subjects. All saw permanency as the ideal, though several did not behave in a manner which was supportive of the marriage. However, an element of change is evident in that separation is now an option, even if reluctantly chosen. The restriction of child bearing to marriage continues to be a significant guide to behaviour. Many pregnant women married to ensure that their children would be born within marriage and most of those who became mothers prior to marriage, married within a short time of the birth.[3] Arensberg and Kimball depicted women as the emotional centre of the family. This finds a reflection in the fact that the current emphasis on emotional fulfilment is most pronounced among women and that mothers continue to be the principal carers for children. Men persist in having a more traditional, detached view of marriage. Paradoxically, an element of continuity is also evident in the fact that people opt to apply to the Tribunal. Their enduring belief in marriage is apparent in their wish to have the option of obtaining sacramental form for a current or hoped-for subsequent relationship.

COMPARISON WITH OTHER LITERATURE

In this study we have tried to enhance our understanding of the phenomenon of the increasing number of Irish people who are disengaging from marriage. Therefore, it is useful to compare and contrast our findings with studies of marriage and the family conducted in Ireland and abroad.

Pre-marriage

The literature on marriage breakdown in Ireland is largely focused on the experience of marriage and the problems that led to breakdown. References to premarital factors are sparse. Arensberg and Kimball depicted the Irish system of spousal selection up to the middle of the present century as impersonal and patriarchal in nature. Change was evident in the studies conducted by Messenger, McNabb, Brody, Humphries, O'Higgins (1974) and Hannan and Katsiaouni. The present study confirms the continuation of the trends described by these authors which is particularly evident in the fact that spousal selection is now an individual matter for the couple concerned. Involvement of parents is apparent only in the area of urging the upgrading of the relationship from informal to marital in selected crisis situations, such as premarital pregnancy. However, the original choice of the partner is at the discretion of the couple themselves. Curtin commented on the tendency of people to marry partners that resemble themselves and this is confirmed by this study.[4] This similarity was also evident in our study in demographic, social, educational, and geographic terms.

Murphy's assertion that dysfunctional families of origin are associated with unstable marriages is supported by the present study.[5] His contention that duration of courtship and age at marriage are not infallible indicators of success or failure in marriage is supported by the present study. Our findings support O'Higgins' conclusion that 'it is not the length of the courtship ... that is important, but the degree of friendship attained in the time'.[6] Our study also reinforces her depiction of courtship as a process of 'going through the motions' for many participants.[7] We noted our subjects' failure to make adequate preparation for marriage in terms of savings and/or accommodation. O'Higgins' statement that this lack indicated an 'attitude of not seeing beyond the marriage ceremony and their lack of understanding of the commitment involved',[8] also serves as a summary of our findings. Our findings concur with Murphy's conclusion that a premarital pregnancy does not, of itself, cause a dysfunctional marriage.[9] However, it does contribute in a negative fashion when combined with other factors such as early marriage, short courtships and dysfunctional families of origin.

Considerable American and Canadian research had been conducted regarding issues such as sexual activity and cohabitation prior to marriage. Their thesis that cohabitation does not reduce the risk of failure in a subsequent marriage resonates with our findings. The conclusion that for American white women, cohabitation is a transitional stage to marriage, also appeared to be true for the members of our sample.[10]

Marriage

Our findings regarding the current understanding of marriage are best summarised by Hannan and Katsiaouni in their 1970s Irish study:

> The marital relationship has become increasingly based on emotionally supportive bonds built up between couples in the courtship and early marriage stage, and has been moving away from the almost instrumental basis of the relationship which appeared to be characteristic of traditional marriages.[11]

In 1994 Whelan and Fahey published their analysis of Irish couples' expectations of marriage. They concluded that affection, mutual respect, faithfulness, understanding and tolerance are regarded by Irish people as the most important factors in a successful marriage.[12] This analysis is in line with our finding that the quality of the interpersonal relationship is now regarded as the core element in a successful marriage. In our sample, breakdown occurred when these expectations, particularly on the part of woman, were not met.

Alcohol abuse

Our findings reflect those of Murphy, who stated 'Alcoholism is a well-known destroyer of marriages and impinges on practically every aspect of family life.'[13] O'Higgins concurs: '[drink] manifests itself as one of the main areas of conflict in the marriages of our subjects'.[14] Her depiction of excessive drinking as primarily a male problem also concurs with our findings. Our conclusions also tally with the link that Murphy, O'Higgins and others posit between alcohol abuse and domestic violence, unhappy families of origin, and pre-marital pregnancies.

Sexual issues

O'Higgins' description of her subjects' understanding of sex as more than merely a means of reproduction, is confirmed in our study.[15] The increased availability and use of artificial birth control in recent decades has permitted the pleasurable aspect of sex to be further emphasised. We noted the contrast between her subjects' reticence to discuss the sexual aspect of their marriage with the openness demonstrated by our subjects. This reflects the decline in sex as a taboo subject in the intervening years. Our findings are also in line with Colgan McCarthy's comment that 'Wives, by and large, favour greater degrees of intimacy and closeness over sex, while men frequently regard sex as more significant.'[16] Our finding that sexual problems serve as barometers of the broader marital relationship is consistent with O'Higgins' and Colgan McCarthy's comments.[17]

Violence

Our findings regarding violence conflict with those of O'Higgins. She concluded that:

> Violence had no major significance for our subjects. It was a problem for some, but not an insurmountable one. Though not acceptable to the subjects, it was only problematic for a very small number.[18]

Perhaps the twenty-year gap between O'Higgins' research and the present study, and the more confident attitude which is characteristic of contemporary women in relationships, is relevant in explaining our differing findings regarding the impact of violence. It is interesting that our findings concur with more recent studies such as Fahey and Lyons' research which was published in 1995. They concluded that:

> Domestic violence seems to have been the single most common precipitating factor behind family law cases appearing in the Irish courts.[19]

For our subjects, violence was also a crisis issue and was a major factor in the breakdown of the marriages concerned.

Children

Our finding that children are regarded as discretional rather than providential[20] is in line with several studies.[21] Nic Ghiolla Phádraig's 1984 study contained evidence that contraception was a moral issue for many people.[22] In contrast, our study reflects the changed situation as expressed by Lee and by Nic Ghiolla Phádraig and Clancy in their 1995 article: that the use of all forms of contraception is now an accepted part of Irish life.[23] Our sample is too small to permit sustainable conclusions regarding abortion. However, while our findings do not contradict the thesis that it is becoming increasingly accepted, at least in some circumstances, yet for our subjects abortion continues to have a moral dimension.

Our findings are in line with the findings of O'Higgins and others[24] that the rearing of children was primarily a female responsibility. A continuation with traditional Irish practices as outlines by Arensberg and Kimball in the 1930s study is evident in this regard. O'Higgins concluded that children impact on the marriage in her sample by severely limiting the couple's social life.[25] In common with the present study, she failed to establish a link between the date of birth of the couple's last child and the date of separation. Our finding that children pose an additional strain on a marriage is supported by the 1994 Accord, Dublin report.[26] Paradoxically, we also found that children can serve as a disincentive to separation, in that they may increase the determination of at least one parent to continue in the marriage.

Communication

Communication was the main problem area in the marriages in our sample. Failure in communication is synonymous with breakdown in the current understanding of marriage in Ireland. This finding is in line with the experience of the counselling agencies, as outlined in their annual reports. O'Higgins reached a similar conclusion. She states: 'during the existence of this marriage this same inability to communicate continued'.[27] International research presents similar findings.[28]

Gender issues

A key factor in our study are the changed role and expectations of women. The contrast with Irish society prior to the 1950s is stark. Evidence of change in this regard was reported by Hannan and Katsiaouni who noted that frequently women had different expectations of marriage than men and this led to conflict.[29] This concurs with our finding that women attached more importance to the emotional aspect of marriage, while men retained a more impersonal view.[30] The greater personal freedom available to women due to their greater assertiveness and increased economic self-reliance, was found to be a significant factor in our study. This reflects the findings of Fahey.[31] Thomas' 1949 study of American Catholics contains similar findings to the present one. He found that the new role of women in society, and their desire to achieve greater independence and equality, has resulted in women becoming less tolerant of disappointment in marriage.[32] He concluded that 'it is the wife who feels the greatest need to have her changed marital status approved by the church'.[33] This is in line with our finding that the majority of our petitioners were female. Thomas goes on to say:

> The present trend towards greater female equality and independence for women, implying as it does a weakening of the foundations upon which the prerogatives of male dominance in marriage were based, has led many wives to be less tolerant and long suffering than they have been. Contrary to the past, many prefer to support themselves and even their children than to put up with abusive, drunken or unfaithful husbands ... The crux of the problem in such cases is that husbands are loath to re-define their roles.[34]

Reflecting Thomas' conclusions, we also found in the present study that women were most likely to be the discontented partner in marriage and were also most likely to take action to precipitate separation.

Values

A decline in a Catholic Church inspired understanding of life is evident in religious practice and sexual morality. The findings of Whelan and Fahey regarding the growth in individual choice are reflected in our study. Corish has written of the ending of the traditional alliance between women and the church.[35] This is particularly evident in women's independent approach to decision-making regarding appropriate sexual behaviour. Corish's point regarding the continuing attachment of the Irish to the church as a body of spiritual beliefs, is evident in the desire of people to have the situation regarding the ending of their marriage regularised in the eyes of the church. The change and continuity evident in the literature is reflected in our study. Enhanced individual choice co-exists with ongoing attachment to religious faith.

Separation

Our findings reflect those of O'Higgins that women were more likely than men to avail of counselling or other help.[36] The reports from the various counselling agencies support this contention. Our findings are also in line with Fahey and Lyons' conclusion that post-separation, children reside with their mother in the overwhelming majority of cases.[37] Our findings were also in general agreement with these authors' conclusion that the woman is most likely to continue residing in the family home.

Our study supports the view that no single cause explains the failure of a marriage. O'Higgins summarised her study by stating that 'Desertion for our subjects is the result of a piling up of adverse situations.'[38] Thomas' view that personal factors play an important role in marriage is also borne out in our study. He stated:

It should be noted that some couples achieve happiness under circumstances that lead to disruption in others, so that it is not what happens but to whom it happens that seems most decisive.[39]

In our study, the lack of a control group rendered it impossible to adjudicate between the role played by personal and sociological factors. However, it is clear that both played a role. The problems experienced by most of our couples would place any marriage under major strain, and additionally, at least one partner in each marriage was particularly ill-equipped to cope with the pressure on the marital relationship.

Second relationships

A contrast with O'Higgins' study is evident here. In her all-female study, 10% of her subjects had a male friend, while only 2.5% (one person) was cohabiting.[40] This contrasts with the fact that 65% of women in our study had entered a new relationship.

Considerable social change is evident here. However, the genesis of this change in attitude and practice is perhaps present in the fact that 41% of O'Higgins' subjects expressed some openness to the idea of re-marriage.[41] The finding in American studies, that people in second marriages are more likely than average to experience separation or divorce, finds a resonance in the problems experienced by our subjects in new relationships.[42]

Conclusion

Our study indicates that individual choice is a major feature of our subjects' approach to marriage. This is evident in spousal selection, the nature of the premarital relationship, the role of each spouse within marriage and the availability of the option of leaving the marriage. While people continue to marry within the context of a cultural preference for monogamous, exclusive, lifelong and fruitful marriages, nevertheless the available options are greatly increased. The traditional framework persists but in a much looser form. The cultural straight-jacket dominant in the world depicted by Arensberg and Kimball is now more akin to a loose fitting garment. The externals have remained the same – people still make the same promises on their wedding day as their forebears. However, the lived reality is very different. The transition to a more pliable approach to marriage entailed inevitable problems and our study details many of these adjustment pains.

IMPLICATIONS FOR AGENCIES CONCERNED WITH MARRIAGE

The implications of this study impact on two levels: those outlined above and recommendations concerning possible ameliorating action. A persistent theme of our study has been the inability or unwillingness of spouses to successfully negotiate mutually satisfactory roles in marriage. While much of this deficiency may be due to personal factors, an important role can be played by the agencies that are concerned with marriage. In this section, we shall outline possible implications for the church and for state agencies concerned with marriage.

Church

This study was based on the records of a Catholic Church agency. We noted previously that the Catholic Tribunal system was effectively the only agency available to separated people to effect dissolution of their marriages.[43] Nevertheless, people who approach the tribunal do so out of choice; there is no legal imperative involved. The fact that the people concerned made the approach and facilitated a detailed and prolonged investigation of the circumstances of their marriage, indicated that their membership of the church and the religious dimension of their lives was important for them.

However, our subjects' attachment to the church did not extend to the meaningful observance of significant areas of church teaching. Due to the nature of this study, the area of relationships and sexual morality emerged as central. Extramarital sexual involvement was a marked feature of our subjects' behaviour, encompassing sexual involvement prior to marriage, infidelity during marriage, and involvement in new sexual relationships after separation. We noted the lack of reference to a moral dimension to extramarital sex among the members of our sample. However, in most cases, the general principle of linking sexual intimacy to a commitment between the couple continues to hold true. Casual or promiscuous sexual involvement only characterised a minority. However, the Catholic principle that the commitment required for sexual intercourse is marriage is in practice widely rejected.

A non-adherence to Catholic teaching was also evident in our subjects' approach to marriage as a lived reality. The Catholic understanding of marriage finds its most authoritative, recent expression in Vatican II which described marriage as 'an intimate community of life and love'.[44] However, while our subjects adhered to this vision of marriage in the abstract, a similar commitment was not evident in the practical realm. Flawed preparation and inadequate adjustment by many participants on entry into marriage are evidence of this practical non-observance of church teaching. Other areas in which church teaching was rejected included the virtual elimination of the providential element in procreation. Religious liturgical practice has also declined and references to finding consolation in prayer were rare. The fact that separation is now considered more readily than previously could also constitute a challenge to the Catholic vision of marriage, which stresses permanence and a modicum of self-sacrifice.

In the area of marriage, the church has focused its efforts on providing pre-marriage courses and counselling for couples experiencing difficulties. We noted the shortcomings in pre-marriage courses as identified by our subjects, and the unrealised potential of meetings between priests and couples prior to marriage. However, it is important to set realisable objectives for short courses or meetings, such as those attended by our couples. It is unlikely that any course, no matter how well focused or presented, could overcome the personal or relational shortcomings evident in many of our subjects or their relationships. There is also a problem regarding the acceptability of seeking remedial counselling when problems arise in marriage. A strategy to counteract this aversion to counselling is necessary.

We noted previously that engagement frequently did not entail a significant change in the interpersonal aspects of our couples' relationships. The impact of engagement was frequently restricted to a public commitment to marry, the wearing of a ring by the woman, and an increased likelihood of greater physical intimacy and cohabitation. An increase in the level of discussion by the couples of their future, or a deepening in their relationship, was frequently absent. This trend to restrict the implications of engagement to the sexual and the public, forms part of the broader tendency to drift into marriage with inadequate reflection. A possible strategy to counteract this tendency is the introduction of a formal, public celebration of engagement. This event could take place at a set interval before the marriage ceremony and focus on emphasising the process involved in the couple building their relationship and

discussing their future. While such a public celebration could deni-
grate into a merely social event, or into a semi-formal approval to
commence cohabitation, yet it has the potential to restore engagement as the final and most intense stage of preparation for marriage. Ideally, such an event would alert the couple to the serious
nature of the commitment inherent in marriage and provoke reflection and discussion on their parts. The formal preparation for marriage could be linked to the public celebration of engagement and
provide outside help to the couple as they explore the nature of
their relationship.

Inevitably, such a process would result in some couples deciding
not to marry. However, a more difficult situation would emerge if a
couple or individual refused to take the process seriously or insisted
on marrying despite the presence of serious problems in their relationship. The Catholic Church has traditionally upheld the right of its
members to marry in church. The increasing level of marriage breakdown, and particularly our finding that the problems that undermined many marriages in our sample were frequently present in
courtship, constitute an argument for reviewing this policy. Some
conditions are already attached to the right to marry in church; existing requirements refer to age, consanguinity, the giving of advance
notice and attendance at a recognised pre-marriage course. An additional condition regarding the couple's readiness for marriage could
be added. A difficulty is that the existing conditions are tangible and
easily adjudicated, while the concepts of an appropriate relationship
or degree of maturity for marriage are nebulous. However, a precedent exists in that people who have received church decrees of nullity
may be required to undertake a programme of counselling to address
a particular problem in their lives prior to being permitted to undergo another ceremony of marriage in church. Also, considering the
degree of expertise accumulated by ACCORD and other counselling
agencies, it should be possible to detect the presence of serious warn-
ing signs as couples undergo formal preparation for marriage.

While the above proposals should prove beneficial, a focus on
the central issue is required to achieve significant results. The fact
that most people, in theory at least, adhere to the Catholic view of

marriage as 'the living out in love' of their marital promises[45] is a promising starting point. The primary task is to convert this theoretic adherence into appropriate practical action. This requires a move from an almost exclusively romantic, unrealistic approach to marriage to one which encompasses a modicum of practical understanding. Faith in the all conquering power of love needs to be complemented by greater rationality and practicality. This requires a less superficial approach to courtship, greater exercise of discretion in selecting a marriage partner, and a greater resolve to adopt a lifestyle that is not injurious to the marital relationship. The current partnership concept of marriage requires specific skills in the area of compromise and negotiation on the part of both spouses.

The church has many opportunities to induce the required change in thinking. Most Irish people receive their primary and secondary education in church managed schools. This affords the church the opportunity to encourage the development of the required skills from an early age. Despite the recent decline in practice, the majority of people continue to attend Sunday Mass and other services and this affords the church an opportunity to reinforce the practical implications of marriage, understood as a partnership.

Credibility is fundamental to this task. Automatic acceptance of authority has receded in favour of a selective approach to church teaching. Contemporary experience-based testimony carries more weight than that based on abstract doctrine or inherited wisdom. Consequently, married members of the church are likely to be most effective in communicating ecclesial teaching in this area. Married people have accumulated vast reserves of practical wisdom regarding marriage which would serve to give church teaching in this area a firm grounding in the lived reality of the sacrament. Their involvement in this and other areas of the church's work also resonates with the renewed understanding of baptism and of the nature of the church in Catholic theology. In the past, church initiatives in the area of marriage and the family have been handicapped by an undue emphasis on what contemporary culture regards as peripheral issues, particularly methods of birth control and the civil

law on the dissolution of marriage. A focus on the points of inter-
section between church teaching and contemporary culture,
emphasising a positive vision, is most likely to prove effective. A
concentration on the features of current practice which conflict with
church teaching has not proved fruitful. The basic conformity
between the church's view of marriage and that of contemporary
society, along with the persistent, even if in some cases residual,
attachment to the faith makes the task achievable.

State agencies

Since the introduction of civil registration, secular authorities have
had a role in marriage. The Irish state has concerned itself with matters such as the age for entry into marriage, the protection of spouses,
specific taxation provisions for married couples, inheritance rights,
and the mechanisms by which couples can separate, annul and
most recently dissolve their marriages. The state has been involved
in areas such as the education and welfare of children, care of the
sick and other matters which were formerly the realm of the family.
The state has also a concern for the stability of family life which is
expressed in the constitution[46] and reiterated in political and official policy statements.[47] A link between unstable family life and
problems such as neglect or abuse of children, juvenile delinquency,
alcohol and drug abuse, crime and general anti-social behaviour, is
widely accepted by state agencies.

Traditionally, the state has played little direct role in supporting
marriage. This is extraordinary in view of the contents of the Irish
constitution. Perhaps the informal alliance between church and
state which was a feature of Irish civil society until recently, was a
factor here.[48] The church undertook responsibility for marriage as a
social arrangement, while the state looked after the fiscal and legislative aspects. The 1996 divorce referendum was characterised by
commitments on the part of political leaders regarding greater state
involvement in support of marriage. Some progress has been made
in this regard including increased funding for counselling and
mediation services[49] and the establishment of a family affairs unit
in a department of state.[50]

Possible further action on the part of the state includes enhanced support for research on the family. We have previously noted the dearth of our knowledge in this area. Appropriate policy decisions require relevant information. Scientific research into the causes of increasing instability in marriage and family life requires considerable resources. A major shortcoming in the present study is the lack of a control group. All the marriages in our sample ended in separation. A parallel study of marriages that functioned to the satisfaction of both parties would allow us to focus on the skills required to overcome marital problems. Not all marriages affected by problems such as alcohol abuse or infidelity experience breakdown. Our study has demonstrated that our couples lacked the skills necessary to overcome these difficulties. The use of a control group would allow us more clearly to delineate the positive qualities required on individual and relationship levels to ensure success in marriage.

Research could fruitfully focus on formal premarital preparation. A study focused on how premarital preparation could serve to alert couples to problems in their relationship and/or in their own personal approach to marriage, would be beneficial. A study based on interviews with couples about to marry and those married for five years would greatly enhance our knowledge of the most effective content and presentation of pre-marriage courses. Other aspects of formal preparation for marriage, such as the meetings between the couple and the priest, could also be profitably included.

A longitudinal, ongoing study would meet the above requirements and serve to address numerous lacunae in our knowledge of marriage and the family. Such a study, beginning pre-marriage and repeated at five year intervals, would permit us to trace the development of the couples' relationships over an extended period. Expectations and reality could be compared. The satisfaction and performance of both parties could also be reviewed. It would also allow us to compare the family backgrounds, courtships and other relevant factors of couples who find happiness in marriage and those who experience breakdown. A focus on the development of emotionally-supportive bonds between the couples would be particularly helpful. A longitudinal study would also permit us to compare the impact of various types of parental marital relationships on children. This would enhance our understanding of recently debated questions such as the relative effect on children of their parents separating or opting to continue in an unsatisfactory marriage. The impact of new relationships on children and the participants could also be studied. The difficulty with such a study is the high requirement in terms of resources. Kiely has noted that the emergence of the economic institution as the pivotal one in Irish society has been mirrored in an similar focus in sociological research.[51] While research on issues such as poverty and unemployment has provided valuable insights, a broader focus is necessary. The important role played by the family in our society and the necessity to devise appropriate policies and initiatives to support it amply justifies the expenditure of the necessary resources.

Regarding its wider role in society, the state is assuming an increasing role in education, particularly in the areas of relationships and sexuality. This affords the state an opportunity to promote a more realistic approach to marriage.[52] A public awareness campaign also may be appropriate in combating the resistance to counselling, both as a preparation for marriage and as a strategy to deal with problems in marriage. Such campaigns have been used in regard to other matters of public concern.[53] The limited nature of non-church counselling agencies is also a discrepancy. Many people may not wish to approach a church agency, yet in many areas of the country there is no alternative available. We previously discussed the detrimental impact of bitterness between the couple, post separation. The promotion of mediation, as an alternative to the adversarial court system, would prove beneficial in reducing this bitterness. Consideration of the impact of government fiscal and legislative policy is beyond our scope.[54] However, an examination of all fiscal and legislative measures for their impact on the family, prior to implementation, would prove beneficial. A unit within an appropriate department of state could review all proposed legislation and provide a critique of its likely impact on the stability of marriage and the family.[55] The investment in time and resources is justifiable in the context of the priority attached to a stable family life, by the Irish constitution and government policy.

The most common single factor which undermined the marriages in our sample was the abuse of alcohol. While it is possible to debate its aetiology and possible association with personal shortcomings and social failure in other areas of life, the inescapable conclusion of this and other studies is that alcohol abuse seriously undermines marriage.[56] In the past the state has sought to encourage certain forms of consumption and discourage others, most notable the campaign to discourage smoking. It could be argued that the damage to society caused by alcohol abuse is considerable, since not only the abuser but also his/her spouse, children and family are affected. Alcohol abuse is also associated with low productivity in work, violent and other anti-social behaviour. Efforts by the state to curb excessive drinking have to date focused on the dangers of driving while under the influence of alcohol. A broader focus is required. In the past, the church took the lead in addressing the issue of intemperance.[57] However, as the appeal of religious inspired crusades diminishes, there is a need for the state to highlight the impact of alcohol abuse on personal health, stability of marriage, family life and economic well-being.

WHAT WILL THE FUTURE HOLD?

The future is always an unknown quantity. The element of surprise may be little or great but it will always be present. When it comes to talking about matters as intricate as human relationships, the unpredictable looms especially large.

Marriage has been a feature of Irish society since earliest times and it is unlikely to disappear from our culture. However, it is difficult to foretell the form that marriage will take in the future. In every aspect of human life, there is always a tension between the institutional, rigid, formal aspects and the more fluid, personal features. In marriage, the institutional consists in values such as fidelity, belief in marriage as a lifelong commitment and openness to children, and these in turn depend on a willingness to make personal sacrifices for the sake of the relationship and to defer immediate gain for the longer term mutual benefit of the couple. The personal aspects are the personal satisfaction and benefits that the marital relationship brings to the participants. An excessive emphasis on the formal features of an institution results in a dry, meaningless though orderly experience for the participants. Conversely, to accord undue prominence to the personal aspects leads to instability and uncontrolled fluctuation.

The search for an appropriate balance between the institutional and the personal will continue to be a feature of marriage and relationships in Ireland in the future. The under-valuation of the personal which was a feature of the past has been rejected by Irish people. However, the present study shows that we are in danger of excessively compensating by over-focusing on the personal. Virtually all the trends which have been discussed in this study point in this direction. Since extreme situations frequently lead to excessive responses, it is not altogether surprising that the current Irish understanding of marriage stresses the personal at the expense of the formal aspects. However, a modicum of stability is a key requirement in the attainment of happiness in relationships and it is important that our view of marriage encompasses both the institutional and the personal.

A feature of life which has scarcely received a mention in this study is the spiritual aspect. All eighty couples in our study had their marriages solemnised in church and invoked the blessing of Christ as they began their life together. Yet, extremely few contributors to the files on which this study is based referred to religion or to the spiritual aspect of life. While our study consists in an analysis of such information as is available to us, and does not extend to speculation regarding possible lacunae in the files, yet this absence is noteworthy. Loving, human relationships, of which marriage is the prime example, involve reaching out beyond oneself so that two lives and hearts may become entwined. The material and the physical may take people some way along this journey, but only that which is distinctively human, the spirit, will make its attainment complete.

Notes

CHAPTER ONE

1. For a discussion of the impact of the famine on Irish family patterns, cf. K. H. Connell, *Irish Peasant Society* (Oxford: Claredon Press, 1968) pp. 113-161.
2. Conrad M. Arensberg and Solon T. Kimball *Family and Community in Ireland* (Harvard University Press, Cambridge University Press, 1940).
3. The most important of these studies include John C. Messenger, *Inis Beag Isle of Ireland* (New York: Holt, Rinehart and Winston, 1969); Patrick McNabb, 'Demography' and 'Social Structure' in Jeremiah Newman (Ed), *The Limerick Rural Survey* (Tipperary: Muintir Na Tire, 1964) pp. 158-247; Hugh Brody, *Inishkillane Change and Decline in the West of Ireland*, (London: Jill Norman, & Hobhouse) 1982 Edition. Originally published by Allen Lane, London, 1973 and Damian F. Hannan and Louise A. Katsiaouni, *Traditional Families? From Culturally Prescribed to Negotiated Roles in Farm Families* (Dublin: E.S.R.I. Paper No. 87, 1977).
4. Hannan and Katsiaouni, op. cit.
5. ibid., pp. 183-184.
6. Examples include Deirdre Kirke, 'Unmarried Mothers: A Comparative Study' in *Economic and Social Review*, Vol. 10, No. 2, (January, 1979) pp. 157-167 and Kathleen O'Higgins, *Family Problems – Substitute Care: Children in Care and their Families* (Dublin: E. S. R. I., 1993).
7. O'Higgins *Family Problems – Substitute Care: Children in Care and their Families* (Dublin: E.S.R.I., 1993), pp. 8-10.
8. Kathleen O'Higgins, *Marital Desertion in Dublin: An Exploratory Study* (Dublin: E. S. R. I., 1974.).
9. ibid., p. 40.
10. ibid., p. 135.
11. Eamonn Murphy, 'Understanding Dysfunctional Marriages' (Unpublished Article, Galway Family Guidance Institute, 1992).
12. The Common Market later evolved into the European Union.
13. Marguerite Corish, 'Aspects of the Secularisation of Irish Society (1958-1996),' in Eoin G. Cassidy, (Ed) *Faith and Culture in the Irish Context* (Dublin: Veritas, 1996) pp. 138-172.
14. For an analysis of changing demographic trends in Ireland, c.f Patrick Clancy, 'Irish Nuptiality and Fertility Patterns in Transition' in Gabriel Kiely and Valerie Richardson, (Eds), *Family Policy; European Perspectives* (Dublin: Family Studies Centre, UCD, 1991) p. 10.

15 cf. Maire Nic Ghiolla Phádraig, 'Social and Cultural Factors in Family Planning,' in Gabriel Kiely, (Ed) *The Changing Family* (Dublin: Family Studies Unit, UCD, 1984) pp. 58-97. Other authors have also commented on these trends; cf. J.J. Lee *Ireland 1912-1985 Politics and Society* (Cambridge: Cambridge University Press, 1989), p. 656 and Finola Kennedy, *Family, Economy and Government in Ireland*.(Dublin: E. S. R. I., 1989) pp. 41-42.

16. For a discussion of this area, cf. Valerie Richardson, 'The Family Life Styles of Some Single Parents in Ireland' in Gabriel Kiely (Ed), *In and Out of Marriage* (Dublin: Family Studies Centre, UCD 1992) pp. 70-86.

17. The 1993 figure is quoted by Maire Nic Ghiolla Phádraig and Patrick Clancy 'Marital Fertility and Family Planning' in Imelda Colgan McCarthy, (Ed), *Irish Family Studies: Selected Papers* (Dublin: Family Studies Centre, UCD 1995) p. 88.

18. Tony Fahey and Maureen Lyons, *Marital Breakdown and Family Law in Ireland* (Dublin: Oak Tree Press, 1994) pp. 97-110.

19. Clancy, art. cit.

20. Donald Connery, *The Irish* (London: 1968) pp. 130-131, quoted in J.H. Whyte, *Church and State in Modern Ireland 1923-1979* (Dublin: Gill and Macmillan, Second Edition, 1980). Originally published in 1971, p. 5.

21. Donal Murray, *Secularism and the New Europe* (Dublin: Veritas, 1990) p. 5.

22. The graph is based on various surveys quoted by Marguerite Corish, art. cit. pp. 156-157. The figures include all those who attend Mass at least once a week.

23. Michael P. Homsby-Smith and Christopher T. Whelan, 'Religious and Moral Values' in Christopher T. Whelan (Ed), *Values and Social Change in Ireland* (Dublin: Gill and Macmillan, 1994) pp. 7-44.

24. Social issues in this context refers to issues of inequality and poverty.

25. cf. *Irish Catholic Directory 1996* (Dublin: Veritas, 1996) p. 249.

26. This figure is accurate at February 1997. It is likely that a small number of the remaining 1993 cases may yet each decision stage.

27. For a discussion of this point, cf. Alicia Sloan, 'Annulment – Divorce For Catholics?' in *Studies* Vol. 87 No. 345, (Summer, 1998) pp. 51-56. She argues that most approaches to the tribunal are motivated by a desire to receive the sacraments again and that people motivated by spiritual reasons are unlikely to lie under oath. She adds that the decline in the social stigma associated with living in a union not recognised by the Catholic Church, has removed the motivation for seeking an annulment for non-spiritual reasons. She feels that the use of witnesses and professional evidence permits the tribunal to identify attempts to misrepresent the facts. Sloan is writing in a British context and it is likely that some residual stigma towards irregular unions persists in the more traditional areas served by the Galway Tribunal.

CHAPTER TWO

1. When an application is received by the tribunal, a preliminary judgement is made regarding the possible existence of a case for the granting of a decree nullity. If the tribunal judges believe that there is very little likelihood of proving nullity in this case, the applicant is advised to withdraw the application. While some persist with the application most accept the tribunal's advice.

2. Fahey and Lyons (op. cit. p. 66) report a similar imbalance in the civil arena. In their sample, drawn from the civil legal system, women took the initiative in 72% of cases.

3. O'Higgins found a similar trend in her 1974 Dublin based study. However, due to the high number of Irish people who move to Dublin to work, one-third of her sample members were born outside Dublin. cf. *Marital Desertion* ... pp. 21-22.

4. The figures reported by Fahey and Lyons in their study of marital cases in the civil legal system are broadly similar: cf. op. cit. p. 52. They state that in their sample 67% of males were at work, 25% unemployed, 1% home duties and 7% 'other'. For women the equivalent figures were 49% employed; 13% unemployed; 33% home duties and 5% 'other'.

5. cf. Corish, art. cit. pp. 156-157. This information is presented in Figure 1.1 above.

6. cf. Christopher T. Whelan and Tony Fahey, 'Religious Change in Ireland 1981-1990' in Eoin G. Cassidy, (Ed), *Faith and Culture in the Irish Context* (Dublin: Veritas, 1996) pp. 101-102.

7. Clancy found that in 1986 the average age on marriage in Ireland was 27.6 years for men and 25.6 years for women, op. cit. p. 12.

8. Murphy posits a link between pre-marital pregnancy and early marriage. cf. Murphy (1992), art. cit.

9. Murphy (1992) art. cit. p. 18. O'Higgins' research supports Murphy's finding. cf. *Marital Desertion...* pp. 28-30.

10. This finding contrasts somewhat with the findings of Fahey and Lyons in their study of cases processed under Irish family law. They report that two thirds of their sample had relationships of eleven years or more, and a quarter were together for twenty-one years or more. cf. Fahey and Lyons, op. cit. pp. 47-48.

11. O'Higgins, *Marital Desertion...* pp. 58-59.

12. O'Higgins, *Marital Desertion...* p. 108.

CHAPTER THREE

1. Murphy (1992), art. cit. pp. 17-18. In Murphy's study, 51% of males and 39% of females claimed that their upbringing left them insecure and emotionally ill-equipped to face adult life. Murphy regards this as one of the main causes of instability in marriage. cf. ibid. p. 17. In our study the equivalent percentages are 36.2% for men and 35% for women.

2. cf. Eamon Murphy, 'The Experience of Sexual Abuse in Childhood' (Galway Family Guidance Institute, 1991, Unpublished). Murphy bases his study on a sample of forty people of whom thirty-six were female. He refers to the 'distorted perceptions it [child sexual abuse] gave its victims about society, about intimate others, about sexuality ... [about] themselves ... some had fallen into ... promiscuity ... Many [women] felt no sexual emotion during their marriages', p. 18.

3. The attitudes presented in Hyde's study on contraceptive attitudes among unmarried mothers find a resonance in our data. cf. Abbie Hyde, 'Unmarried Pregnant Women's Accounts Of Their Contraceptive Practices: A Qualitative Analysis' in *Irish Journal of Sociology*, Vol. 6, 1996, pp. 179-211.

4. In many cases, by the time the couple had acquired the requisite financial security, their relationship had deteriorated to the extent that they did not consider it appropriate to have children. However, some such couples opted to have a child in the hope that it would enhance their troubled marriage.

5. For a discussion of this point, cf. Nic Ghiolla Phádraig (1984), art. cit. pp. 58-94.

6. Intention is an internal, mental design which may not always find expression in external acts. Therefore, it is difficult to demonstrate the existence of an intention, at the time of marriage, to exclude any of these elements.

CHAPTER FOUR

1. The following abbreviations are used in Figure 4.1 Sex: Sexual issues; Mon: Financial issues; Infil: Infidelity; Viol: Violence; Alcohol: Alcohol Abuse; Accom: Accommodation; In Laws: Relations with extended family; Gamb: Gambling; Class: Social class; Drugs: Abuse of Drugs; Ed: Education.

2. O'Higgins, *Marital Desertion*... 'As might be expected here there was a general reticence on the part of our subjects to talk about this aspect of their marriages .' p. 80.

3. A male-female dichotomy is apparent here; 11.25% of women are depicted as having a diminished interest in the sexual aspect of the marriage, which contrasts with 3.75% of men.

4. O'Higgins, *Marital Desertion*... pp. 81-82.

5. Accord is a Catholic marriage counselling organisation. The report referred to here was produced by the Dublin diocesan branch of the organisation.

6. Finola Ó Riagáin analyses the profile of those who avail of the services provided by A.I.M. in 'Reasons for Marital Instability and Divorce' in Mags O'Brien, (Ed) *Divorce? Facing the Issues of Marital Breakdown* (Dublin: Basement Press, 1995) p. 32. A.I.M. provides 'non-directive counselling, legal information, a referral and, more recently, a mediation service to people with marriage and family problems'. ibid. p. 27.

7. Murphy (1992), art. cit.
8. Marriage and Relationship Counselling Services, (M.R.C.S.) 1995 Annual Report. M.R.C.S. is a non-denominational, Dublin based agency founded in 1962.
9. Exceptions are A.I.M. and M.R.C.S., some of whose clients seek help in mediating a separation.
10. Murphy (1992), art. cit.
11. Recent unpublished research on clients of M.R.C.S. shows that 24% of male clients and 15% of female clients admitted to being unfaithful. However, Yvonne Jacobson, the author of the research, comments that 'The true figure is probably closer to 60%. Most people who have affairs probably get away with it without anyone finding out.' Jacobson's conclusions and comments are quoted in *The Irish Times*, March 14th, 1998.
12. Exceptions may include cases processed under the heading of intention against fidelity and cases where infidelity is the manifestation of a deeper problem.
13. There is a contrast here with O'Higgins 1974 findings. She concludes 'violence had no major significance for our subjects. Although not acceptable to the subjects it was only problematic for a very small number.' O'Higgins *Marital Desertion...* p. 93.
14. In the overall sample, 30% of women are depicted as unfaithful.
15. Sheila Greene states: 'The presence of children can prevent marriage breakdown, if parents resolve to stay together because of them, but it is also a cause of marriage breakdown when parents are poorly equipped for parenting and where, perhaps, illness or handicap in the child bring extra demands.' cf. Dr Sheila Greene, 'Marital Breakdown and Divorce; The psychological consequences for adults and their children' in Mags O'Brien (Ed), *Divorce? Facing the Issues of Marital Breakdown* (Dublin: Basement Press, 1995) pp. 38-54. The quotation is from p. 52

CHAPTER FIVE

1. O'Higgins in her 1974 study produced a comparable figure of circa 33%, cf. *Marital Desertion...* p. 83.
2. The average duration of marriage for this sub-sample was 7.9 years, which contrasts with 6.2 years for the total sample.
3. O'Higgins *Marital Desertion...* p. 83. O'Higgins does not provide any further statistical analysis.
4. Ó Riagáin, art. cit. pp. 33-34.
5. In the figures in this chapter the following abbreviations will be used to connote the problem areas in marriage. Sex: Sexual issues; Money: financial related problems, V: Violence; A-H: Alcohol abuse by the husband; I-H: Infidelity on the part of the husband; I-W: infidelity on the part of the wife; A: Accommodation; I-L: Problems regarding in-laws and extended family; A-W: Alcohol abuse by the wife; Gamb:

Gambling; Class: Issues relate to social class; Drug: Issues regarding drugs, other than alcohol or tobacco; Ed: Issues concerning education.

6. *Marital Desertion...* p. 95.

7. i.e. The woman terminated the marriage by leaving the family home or by ejecting her husband.

8. Greene states that men who do not 'find a another stable partnership may be at particular risk of isolation and loneliness, since men are often less able than women to establish strong kinship and social networks.' cf. Greene, art. cit. p. 48.

9. *Beginning Experience* is a group based programme, usually organised by the Catholic Church, for people who have lost a partner through bereavement or separation.

10. Clulow has written: 'the impact of a broken marriage depends not only on what has been lost but also on what can be created to take its place.' cf. Christopher Clulow, 'Making, Breaking and Remaking Marriage' in David Clark, (Ed) *Marriage, Domestic Life and Social Change: Writings for Jacqueline Burgoyne* (1944-88) (London and New York: Routledge, 1991) p. 179.

11. Divorce was legislated for in the Republic of Ireland in 1996.

12. Fahey and Lyons, op. cit. pp. 113-123. The authors found that couples at the lower end of the social scale tended to use the protective aspect of Family Law, while those with property used the separation function.

13. cf. Fahey and Lyons, op. cit. p. 94. They found that in 78% of cases the children resided with their mother, 5% with their father, 2% with both equally, 5% some with each parents and 3% with neither. Ward states that 86% of a sample of wives seeking maintenance in the District Court under the 1976 Act had dependant children. cf. Peter Ward, *Divorce in Ireland: Who Should Bear the Cost?* (Cork: Cork University Press, 1993) p. 12.

14. Figure 5.10 is based on the entire sample and includes childless couples. Therefore the percentages differ from those contained in the text.

15. Fahey and Lyons, op. cit. pp. 89-91. In their sample the husband left the family home in 61% of cases, while the wife moved out in 18% of cases and in a further 16% of cases both moved out and the home was disposed of .

16. 58% of these marriages are depicted as violent, as opposed to 46% in the total study.

17. cf. Damian F. Hannan, 'Patterns of Spousal Accommodation and Conflict in Traditional and Modern Farm Families' in *Economic and Social Review*, Vol. 10, No. 1 (October, 1978) pp. 61-84. In this research based study, Hannan finds that men are more likely to have a traditional view of marriage, while women are more likely to stress the shared relationship based aspects.

CHAPTER SIX

1 Pat O'Connor, 'Understanding Continuities and Changes in Irish Marriage: Putting Women Centre Stage' in *Irish Journal of Sociology*, Vol. 4, 1994, p. 150.

2. In this context, sexual problems do not include violence in the sexual area, which is akin to spousal abuse.

3. Since our sample is composed of separated people, all our subjects had opted to marry. However, authors such as F. Kennedy speak of the enduring popularity of marriage, cf. F. Kennedy (1989) passim.

4. Chris Curtin, 'Marriage and Family' in Patrick Clancy, *et al* (Eds), *Ireland: A Sociological Profile* (Dublin: Institute of Public Administration, 1986) p. 159

5. Murphy (1992), art. cit.

6 O'Higgins, *Marital Desertion...* p. 30.

7. ibid., p. 40.

8. ibid., p. 40.

9. Murphy (1992), op. cit. p. 16.

10. Wendy D. Manning, 'Marriage and Cohabitation Following Premarital Conception' in *Journal of Marriage and the Family* , Vol. 55 (November 1993) pp. 839-850.

11. Hannan & Katsiaouni, op. cit. pp. 183-184.

12. cf. Whelan and Fahey (1994), art. cit. pp. 45-81.

13. Murphy (1992), art. cit.

14. O'Higgins, *Marital Desertion...* p. 92.

15. ibid., p. 78.

16. Imelda Colgan McCarthy, 'Marriage Knots: Some Thoughts for Therapists' in Imelda Colgan McCarthy (Ed) I*rish Family Studies: Selected Papers* (Dublin: Family Studies Centre, UCD, 1995) p. 82.

17. Colgan McCarthy states that sex frequently becomes the defining issue in marriages involving situations of inequality. ibid. p. 83.

18. O'Higgins, *Marital Desertion...* p. 93.

19. Fahy and Lyons, op. cit. p. 124.

20. This is clear in O'Higgins' 1974 findings. She states: 'Children just seemed to arrive.' *Marital Desertion...* p. 76. This is indicative of the change in attitude regarding children among Irish couples.

21. Finola Kennedy (1989), op. cit. p. 41, Nic Ghiolla Phádraig (1984), art. cit. passim and Nic Ghiolla Phádraig and Clancy, art. cit. passim.

22. Nic Ghiolla Phádraig (1984) pp. 92-93.

23. J.J. Lee, *Ireland 1912-1985 Politics and Society* (Cambridge: Cambridge University Press, 1989) p. 656. Nic Ghiolla Phádraig and Clancy, art cit.

24. cf. Gabriel Kiely, 'Fathers in Families' in Imelda Colgan McCarthy (Ed), *Irish Family Studies: Selected Papers* (Dublin: Family Studies Centre, UCD, 1995) pp. 147-158. Kiely concludes 'This study shows that the burden of housework and child care clearly falls heaviest on mothers.' art. cit. p. 157.

25. O'Higgins, *Marital Desertion*... pp. 74-78.

26. Dublin Accord, 1994 Report.

27. O'Higgins, *Marital Desertion*... p. 78.

28. cf. Lynn K. White, 'Determinants of Divorce: A Review of Research in the Eighties' in *Journal of Marriage and the Family*, Vol. 52 (November 1990) pp. 904-912.

29. Hannan & Katsiaouni, op. cit. p. 164.

30. Hannan (1978), art cit., concludes 'the hypothesis that wives provide the driving force behind family role modernisation is strongly supported' p. 82. Colgan McCarthy speaks of men in marriage looking outwards while their wives look inwards, cf. Imelda Colgan McCarthy, art cit., p. 83.

31. Fahey, art. cit., pp. 219-222.

32. Thomas, art. cit.

33. John L. Thomas, 'Catholic Family Disorganisation' in Ernest W. Burgess and Donald J. Bogue (Eds), *Contributions to Urban Sociology* (Chicago and London: The University of Chicago Press, 1964)., p. 532.

34. ibid., p. 540.

35. Corish, art. cit.

36. O'Higgins, *Marital Desertion*... pp. 94-95.

37. Fahey and Lyons, op. cit. p. 93-94.

38. O'Higgins, *Marital Desertion*... p. 120.

39. Thomas, art. cit., p. 532.

40. O'Higgins, *Marital Desertion*... p. 108. O'Higgins' respondents were exclusively female.

41. ibid., p. 110 and Table 16, p. 149.

42. Lynn K. Whyte, art. cit., pp. 904-912.

43. The introduction of civil divorce in 1996, provided couples with an alternative or complementary route to dissolve unhappy marriages.

44. *Gaudium et Spes* 48 ß1

45. Catholic Rite of Marriage.

46. Bunreacht na hÉireann art. 41 1, 2.

47. cf. Finola Kennedy (1989) p. 69. Kennedy shows that judicial interpretation of the constitution has emphasised the family as based on marriage.

48. Kiely and Richardson posit a link between the principle of subsidiarity and the non-involvement by the state in most family matters, cf. Gabriel Kiely and Valerie Richardson, 'Family Policy in Ireland' in Imelda Colgan McCarthy, (Ed) *Irish Family Studies; Selected Papers* (Dublin: Family Studies Centre, UCD, 1995) pp. 27-47.

49. Fahey and Lyons also recommended that mediation services be made more widely available, cf. op. cit. pp. 128-130.

50. cf. *The Irish Times*, January 5th, 1998.

51. Gabriel Kiely, 'Family Research in Ireland' in Imelda Colgan McCarthy (Ed) *Irish Family Studies: Selected Papers* (Dublin: Family Studies Centre, UCD, 1995) p. 19. Kiely cites Hannan and Katsiaouni, op. cit., as 'the one outstanding exception' to this trend. p. 22.

52. Sheila Greene states 'Unrealistic expectations of marriage and the opposite sex might be less likely if marriage and relationships were recognised as important subjects for schoolchildren to learn about and discuss.' art. cit., p. 52.

53. Recent examples include the public awareness campaigns relating to cigarette smoking and drink and driving. Accord, Dublin conducted an awareness campaign concerning their services during March, 1997.

54. On this issue, cf. F. Kennedy (1989), op. cit. pp. 87-114.

55. Kiely and Richardson refer to the *ad hoc* nature of Irish Government policy on the family and the absence of a government minister with specific responsibility for the family. cf. art. cit. p. 27. F. Kennedy proposed the establishment of a Family Affairs Unit in the Department of Finance to co-ordinate policy and expenditure programmes concerning the family and to propose new initiatives where appropriate. cf. op. cit. (1989) pp. 3, 147-149.

56. For a discussion of the impact of alcohol abuse on family life, cf. Hilda Loughran, 'Families in Transition: Alcohol Problems and the Family Life Cycle' in Imelda Colgan McCarthy (Ed), *Irish Family Studies: Selected Papers* (Dublin: Family Studies Unit, UCD, 1995) pp. 113-125.

57. The most significant effort by the church to counter excessive drinking occurred in the early and mid-nineteenth century under the leadership of Fr Theobald Mathew. For a discussion of Fr Mathew's temperance crusade, cf. Ignatius Murphy *The Diocese of Killaloe 1800-1850* (Dublin: Four Courts Press, 1992) pp. 362-366. Subsequent efforts included the Pioneer Total Abstinence movement and the virtually compulsory pledge taken by candidates for the sacrament of confirmation to abstain from alcohol until adulthood.

Bibliography

Arensberg, Conrad M. and Kimball, Solon T. *Family and Community in Ireland* (Harvard University Press, Cambridge University Press, 1940).

Booth, Alan, *et al*, 'Belief and Behaviour: Does Religion Matter in Today's Marriage' in *Journal of Marriage and the Family*, vol. 57 (August 1995) pp. 661-671.

Breen, Richard, *et al*, (Eds), *Understanding Contemporary Ireland: State Class and Development in the Republic of Ireland* (Dublin: Gill and Macmillan, 1990).

Brody, Hugh, *Inishkillane: Change and Decline in the West of Ireland* (London: Allen Lane, 1973).

Burgoyne, Jacqueline, 'Afterword Does the Ring Make any Difference? Couples and the private face of a public relationship in post-war Britain' in David Clark, (Ed), *Marriage, Domestic Life and Social Change: Writings for Jacqueline Burgoyne* (1944-88) (London and New York: Routledge, 1991) pp. 235-256.

Burke, Helen, 'Continuity and Change: The Life Cycle of Irish Women in the 1980s' in Gabriel Kiely, (Ed), *The Changing Family* (Dublin: Family Studies Centre, UCD, 1984). pp 39-57.

Cinger, Rand D., *et al*, 'Linking Economic Hardship to Marital Quality and Instability,' *Journal of Marriage and the Family*, vol. 52 (August 1990) pp. 643-656.

Clancy, Patrick, 'Irish Nuptiality and Fertility Patterns in Transition' in Gabriel Kiely and Valerie Richardson, (Eds), *Family Policy: European Perspectives* (Dublin: Family Studies Centre, UCD, 1991) pp. 9-29.

Clulow, Christopher, 'Making, Breaking and Remaking Marriage' in David Clark, (Ed), *Marriage, Domestic Life and Social Change: Writings for Jacqueline Burgoyne 1944-88* (London and New York: Routledge, 1991) pp. 167-187.

Colgan McCarthy, Imelda, 'Marriage Knots: Some Thoughts for Therapists' in Imelda Colgan McCarthy, (Ed), *Irish Family Studies: Selected Papers* (Dublin: Family Studies Centre, UCD, 1995) pp. 75-85.

Connell, K.H., *Irish Peasant Society* (Oxford: Clarendon Press, 1968).

Corish, Marguerite, 'Aspects of the Secularisation of Irish Society (1958-1996),' in Eoin G. Cassidy, (Ed), *Faith and Culture in the Irish Context* (Dublin: Veritas, 1996) pp. 138-172.

Corrigan, Carmel, 'Household Structure in Early Twentieth Ireland', *Irish Journal of Sociology*, vol. 3, 1993, pp. 56-78.

Curtin, Chris, 'Marriage and Family' in Patrick Clancy, *et al*, (Eds), Ireland: A Sociological Profile (Dublin: Institute of Public Administration, 1986) pp. 155-172.

Curtin, Chris & Varley, Anthony, 'Marginal Men? Bachelor Farmers in a West of Ireland Community,' in Chris Curtin, *et al*, (Eds), *Gender in Irish Society* (Galway: Galway University Press, 1987): pp. 287-308.

DeMaris, Alfred and MacDonald, William, 'Premarital Cohabitation and Marital Instability: A Test of the Unconventionality Hypothesis,' *Journal of Marriage and the Family*, vol. 55 (May 1993) pp. 399-407.

DeMaris, Alfred and Roa, K. Vaninadha, 'Premarital Cohabitation and Subsequent Marital Stability in the United States: A Reassessment' *Journal of Marriage and the Family*, vol. 54 (February 1992) pp. 178-190.

Dillon, Michele, *Debating Divorce: Moral Conflict in Ireland* (Kentucky: University Press of Kentucky, 1993).

Duggan, Carmel, 'Farming Women or Farmers' Wives?' in Chris Curtin, *et al*, (Eds), *Gender in Irish Society* (Galway: Galway University Press, 1987) pp. 54-69.

Duncan, William R. and Scully, Paula E., *Marriage Breakdown in Ireland Law and Practice* (Dublin: Butterworth, 1990).

Fahey, Tony, 'State, Family and Compulsory Schooling in Ireland' *The Economic and Social Review*, vol. 23, No. 4, (July, 1992) pp. 369- 395.

Fahey, Tony, 'Family and Household in Ireland,' in Patrick Clancy, *et al*, (Eds), *Irish Society: Sociological Perspectives* (Dublin: Institute of Public Administration, 1995) pp. 227-228.

Fahey, Tony and Lyons, Maureen, *Marital Breakdown and Family Law in Ireland* (Dublin: Oak Tree Press, 1994).

Fitzgerald, David, 'Marriage in Post-Famine Ireland' in Art Cosgrave, (Ed), *Marriage in Ireland*, (Dublin: College Press, 1985) pp. 116-131.

Greene, Dr Sheila, 'Marital Breakdown and Divorce: The psychological consequences for adults and their children' in Mags O'Brien, (Ed), *Divorce? Facing the Issues of Marital Breakdown* (Dublin: Basement Press, 1995) pp. 38-54.

Greenstein, Theodore N., 'Marital Disruption and the Employment of Married Women', *Journal of Marriage and the Family*, vol. 52 (August 1990) pp. 657-676.

Hall, David R and Zhoa, John Z., 'Cohabitation and Divorce in Canada: Testing the Selectivity Hypothesis' *Journal of Marriage and the Family*, vol. 57 (May 1995) pp. 421-427.

Hannan, Damian F., 'Patterns of Spousal Accommodation and Conflict in Traditional and Modern Farm Families,' in *Economic and Social Review*, vol. 10, No. 1. (October, 1978) pp. 61-84.

Hannan, Damian F., and Katsiaouni, Louise A., *Traditional Families? From Culturally Prescribed to Negotiated Roles in Farm Families* (Dublin: E.S.R.I. Paper No. 87, 1977).

Hillard, Betty, 'Changing Theoretical Perspectives in the Sociological Study of the Family' in Imelda Colgan McCarthy, (Ed), *Irish Family Studies: Selected Papers* (Dublin: Family Studies Centre UCD, 1995) pp. 59-73.

Hornsby-Smith, Michael P., and Whelan, Christopher T., 'Religious and Moral Values' in Christopher T. Whelan, (Ed), *Values and Social Change in Ireland* (Dublin: Gill & Macmillan, 1994) pp. 7-44.

Humphreys, Alexander J., *New Dubliners: Urbanisation and the Irish Family* (London: Routledge & Kegan Paul, 1966).

Hyde, Abbie, 'Unmarried Pregnant Women's Accounts Of Their Contraceptive Practices: A Qualitative Analysis' in *Irish Journal of Sociology*, vol. 6, 1996, pp. 179-211.

Hynes, Brid, *Law, Social Morality and Divorce* (Unpublished MA Thesis, UCG, 1992).

Kahn, Joan R., and London, Katheryn A., 'Premarital Sex and the Risk of Divorce' *Journal of Marriage and the Family*, vol. 53 (November 1991) pp. 845-855.

Kennedy, Finola, *Family, Economy and Government in Ireland* (Dublin: E.S.R.I., 1989).

Kennedy, Finola, 'Continuity and Change in Marriage and Family in Ireland: Keynote address at C.M.A.C 25th Celebrations' (Unpublished, 1993).

Kennedy, Robert E., *The Irish Emigration, Marriage and Fertility* (Berkeley: University of California Press, 1973).

Kiely, Gabriel, 'Family Research in Ireland' in Imelda Colgan McCarthy, (Ed), *Irish Family Studies: Selected Papers* (Dublin: Family Studies Centre, UCD, 1995) pp. 11-26.

Kiely, Gabriel, 'Fathers in Families' in Imelda Colgan McCarthy, (Ed), *Irish Family Studies: Selected Papers* (Dublin: Family Studies Centre, UCD, 1995) pp. 147-158.

Kiely, Gabriel, and Richardson, Valerie, 'Family Policy in Ireland' in Colgan McCarthy, Imelda, (Ed), *Irish Family Studies: Selected Papers* (Dublin: Family Studies Centre, UCD, 1995) pp. 27-47.

Kirke, Deirdre, 'Unmarried Mothers: A Comparative Study' in *Economic and Social Review*, vol. 10, No. 2, (January, 1979) pp. 157-167.

Loughran, Hilda, 'Families in Transition: Alcohol Problems and the Family life Cycle' in Imelda Colgan McCarthy, (Ed), *Irish Family Studies: Selected Papers* (Dublin: Family Studies Centre, UCD, 1995) pp. 113-125.

Manning, Wendy D., 'Marriage and Cohabitation Following Premarital Conception' *Journal of Marriage and the Family*, vol. 55 (November 1993) pp. 839-850.

Matthews, Lisa S., *et al*, 'Predicting Marital Instability From Spouse and Observer Reports of Marital Interaction' in *Journal of Marriage and The Family*, vol. 58 (August 1996) pp. 641-655.

McCullagh, Ciaran, 'A Tie that Binds: Family and Ideology in Ireland' in *The Economic and Social Review*, vol. 22, No. 3, (April, 1991), pp. 199-211.

McDonnell, Albert, 'When Strangers Marry', *The Furrow*, vol. 50, No. 2, (February, 1999), pp. 67-76.

McNabb, Patrick, 'Demography' in Jeremiah Newman (Ed), *The Limerick Rural Survey* (Tipperary: Muintir Na Tire, 1964) pp. 158-192.

McNabb, Patrick, 'Social Structure' in Jeremiah Newman (Ed), *The Limerick Rural Survey* (Tipperary: Muintir Na Tire, 1964) pp. 193-247.

Messenger, John C., *Inis Beag Isle of Ireland* (New York: Holt, Rinehart and Winston, 1969).

Murphy, Eamonn, 'The Experience of Sexual Abuse in Childhood' (Unpublished Article, Galway Family Guidance Institute, 1991).

Murphy, Eamonn, 'Understanding Dysfunctional Marriages' (Unpublished Article, Galway Family Guidance Institute, 1992).

Murray, Donal, *Secularism and the New Europe* (Dublin: Veritas, 1990).

Nic Ghiolla Phádraig, Maire, 'Social and Cultural Change in Family Planning' in Gabriel Kiely, (Ed), *The Changing Family* (Dublin: Family Studies Centre, UCD, 1984) pp. 58-97.

Nic Ghiolla Phádraig, Maire, 'Marital Separation in Ireland Situating the Results of Research on the First Three Years of Operation of the Family Mediation Service' in Gabriel Kiely, (Ed) *In and Out of Marriage Irish and European Experiences* (Dublin: Family Studies Centre, UCD, 1992) pp. 6-18.

Nic Ghiolla Phádraig, Maire, and Clancy, Patrick 'Marital Fertility and Family Planning' in Imelda Colgan McCarthy, (Ed), *Irish Family Studies: Selected Papers* (Dublin: Family Studies Centre, UCD, 1995) pp. 87-112.

Nock, Steven L., 'Commitment and Dependency in Marriage' *Journal of Marriage and the Family*, vol. 57 (May 1995) pp. 503-514.

O'Connor, Pat, 'Understanding Continuities and Changes in Irish Marriage: Putting Women Centre Stage' *Irish Journal of Sociology*, Vol. 4, 1994, pp. 136-163.

O'Higgins, Kathleen, *Marital Desertion in Dublin An Exploratory Study* (Dublin: E. S. R. I., 1974).

O'Higgins, Kathleen, *Family Problems - Substitute Care: Children in Care and Their Families* (Dublin: E. S. R. I., 1993).

Ó'Riagáin, Finola, 'Reasons for Marital Instability and Divorce' in Mags O'Brien, (Ed), *Divorce? Facing the Issues of Marital Breakdown* (Dublin: Basement Press, 1995) pp. 25-38.

Richardson, Valerie, 'The Family Life Styles of Some Single Parents in Ireland' in Gabriel Kiely, (Ed), *In and Out of Marriage Irish and European Experiences* (Dublin: Family Studies Centre, UCD, 1992) pp. 70-86.

Riddick, Ruth, 'Irish Abortion Rights: 1992, A Year of Achievement' in *UCG Women's Studies Centre Review*, vol. 2 (Galway: UCG, 1993) pp 147-151.

Sloan, Alicia, 'Annulment – Divorce For Catholics?' in *Studies*, Vol. 87 No. 345, (Summer, 1998) pp. 51-56.

Thomas, John L., *The American Catholic Family* (Englewood Cliff, NJ: Prince-Hall, 1956).

Thomas, John L., 'Catholic Family Disorganisation' in Ernest W. Burgess, and Donald J. Bogue, (Eds), *Contributions to Urban Sociology* (Chicago & London: The University of Chicago Press, 1964) pp. 527-540.

Thomson, Elizabeth & Colella, Ugo 'Cohabitation and Marital Stability: Quality or Commitment?' *Journal of Marriage and the Family*, Vol. 54 (November 1992) pp. 259-267.

Tovey, Hilary, 'Rural Sociology in Ireland: a Review' *Irish Journal of Sociology*, Vol. 2, 1992, pp. 96-121.

Tzebg, Meei-Shenn, 'The Effects of Socio-Economic Heterogamy and Changes on Marital Dissolution for First Marriages' *Journal of Marriage and the Family*, Vol. 54 (August 1992) pp. 609-619.

Walsh, Brendan M., 'Marriage in Ireland in the Twentieth Century' in Art Cosgrove, (Ed) *Marriage in Ireland* (Dublin: College Press, 1985) pp. 132-150.

Ward, Peter, *Divorce in Ireland: Who Should Bear the Cost?* (Cork: Cork University Press, 1993).

Whelan, Christopher T., 'Irish Social Values: Traditional or Modern?' in Christopher T. Whelan, (Ed), *Values and Social Change in Ireland* (Dublin: Gill & Macmillan, 1994) pp. 212-215.

Whelan, Christopher T. 'Values and Social Change' in Christopher T. Whelan, (Ed) *Values and Social Change in Ireland* (Dublin: Gill & Macmillan, 1994) pp. 1-6.

Whelan, Christopher T., and Fahey, Tony, 'Marriage and the Family' in Christopher T. Whelan, (Ed), *Values and Social Change in Ireland* (Dublin: Gill & Macmillan, 1994) pp. 45-81.

Whelan, Christopher T. and Fahey, Tony, 'Religious Change in Ireland 1981-1990' in Eoin G. Cassidy, (Ed) *Faith and Culture in the Irish Context* (Dublin: Veritas, 1996) pp. 100-116.

White, Lynn K., 'Determinants of Divorce: A Review of Research in the Eighties' *Journal of Marriage and the Family*, vol. 52 (November 1990) pp. 904-912.